turn this change into something better.

LENDAGER GROUP

A CHANGEMAKER'S GUIDE TO THE FUTURE

Anders Lendager and Ditte Lysgaard Vind

A CHANGEMAKER'S GUIDE TO THE FUTURE

Copyright © 2018
by Anders Lendager & Ditte Lysgaard Vind
www.achangemakersguidetothefuture.com
ISBN 978-87-970745-2-7

2nd edition

Note: This paperback version has been adapted to
Amazon's KDP printing standards. As such, the
paperback differs slightly from the original design.

Book design by All the Way to Paris

Photo credits to: Rasmus Hjortshøj - COAST Studio

Editor: Johan Schoonhoven

Thanks to: Arkitektgruppen, NREP, Carlsberg,
Metroselskabet, Københavns Kommune, Plastindustrien
& all the Lendagers, especially Janne, Nicholas,
Philip, Thea and Anna Sophie for their assistance
in creating this book.

A special thanks to Realdania for their support in
making this book a reality.

EXECUTIVE SUMMARY

THIS is a changemaker's guide to the future! A book to read, to grasp, and to act on – to ultimately ensure a livable and sustainable future for your business, our planet and humankind.

By combining innovation, circular economy, design, and technology we harness the extraordinary powers of business as a source of good, and make sure we are incentivised to keep on the trajectory of creating a regenerative society for all to thrive in.

We go beyond the traditional notion of economic growth and environmental protection as each other's opposites – instead, we turn the tables and start treating them as natural *prerequisites.* Strategically integrated sustainability makes viable businesses – and viable businesses drive sustainable development. For us, it's that simple.

So, what we provide here is the road-map for regenerative business. We use circular economy as a tool to cater to global demand without compromising on our climate and environment. The key to unlocking this opportunity lies in the combination of circular economy with design and innovation – enabling us to go from idea to value innovation and bringing it to the market. Here growth is not the enemy. On the contrary, we see growth as a powerful driver of the change we wish to see. Just as it has always been in nature. The bigger the business, the bigger the impact – so what matters is what we grow.

As we highlight throughout this book, we can decouple future economic growth from the excessive use of virgin materials and CO_2-emissions, which has, so far, seemed an inevitable precondition for development. Doing so allows us to create a future where good business equals a healthy environment and a prosperous future for all to thrive in. Ensuring that visionary ideas indeed become tangible results.

The reboot is doable – so let's get started!

FOREWORD

If a business leader fails to realise that sustainable management is the only way to survive and prosper as a company in the 21st century, the company will soon be out of business.

In 2018, the world faced Earth Overshoot Day on the 1st of August. That is, the day of the year when humanity's ecological footprint exceeds earth's biocapacity. The day we all start living beyond means. It is said that we need 1.7 planets to keep up with our current behavior, and we will need even more if our global population and middle-class continue to grow with current rates. If we all come to live like Danes, we would need 4.2 planets!

Should the next great human achievement be the creation of another earth to cover our debts? Or should we cut half of all global consumption beginning from tomorrow to attain balance once again?

The answer is neither. The solution to prevent future overshooting is rather to start keeping our products and materials in circulation for as long as possible.

This requires companies to think radically out of the box; to look beyond the linear economy of take, make and dispose. To develop new business models, products and value chains – accelerated through honest collaborations across fields and borders.

'A changemaker's guide to the future' contains the theories, methods and real-life examples of how to do so. And as you'll discover throughout the book, the transition to circular economy should not be seen as a burden to the corporate world; it is a golden opportunity.

Flemming Besenbacher
Professor dr.scient at Aarhus University
Chairman of the Carlsberg Foundation and
Supervisory Board at Carlsberg A/S

Calling all future climate superstars

"But with the withering
of each blossom of the spirit,
whenever, in the storm of
the times, the work of creative
art is scattered, so forever
will new life sprout forth from
the womb of the Earth.
Restlessly, procreative Nature
opens her buds: unconcerned
whether outrageous humanity
(a forever distant race)
should trample
the ripening fruit"

Alexander Von Humbolt, Views of Nature

A WORLD WITHOUT
RESOURCE SCARCITY

Imagine a world without resource scarcity, where our behaviour doesn't have a negative impact on our climate, where waste doesn't exist, where sustainability and growth are each other's prerequisites. To us, this world is real.

Put simply, we created this book because we had to; the issues we address are just too important to our planet, our society and for each one of us personally. Our global population and resource consumption per capita are rising, as well as the demand for food, electricity and housing. More than ever it is time to change the sustainability narrative as well as the structures of our modern society.

Digitalisation, globalisation, urbanisation, the 4th industrial revolution and climate change are transforming the world as we know it.

Our climate is also changing – rapidly – and these trends are closely related. Currently, more consumption, traffic and buildings equate to more climate change. But it doesn't have to be that way. Our work has revealed some exciting findings that we want to share with you and the wider public, **because we believe that together we can turn this change into something better.**

What we see is a world with an abundance of already existing materials. In this book we show you that concrete, bricks, wood, plastic, glass and metal all can be recirculated and become new materials with new functions and increased value. Encouragingly, the opportunity and potential is not limited to the built environment. We see huge potential across all industries. In other words: looking at waste as a resource will change the game for good. And can we let you in on a secret? It's good business.

What we hope to encourage is a smarter mindset. Where we start creating cities and buildings that utilie and value all of their resources – whether these be nature, culture, people, energy or all the materials we currently throw away as waste. Because doing so enables us to create systems and solutions that enhance bio-diversity, sustainable growth and improve the quality of life for our growing population, making increased demand and growth part of the solution.

However, if we are to succeed with this massive transformation it takes collective change. A change of mindset for professionals, industries, businesses, politicians and citizens alike. In this book, we try to enable that change by showing that it is in fact both im-portant and possible to do things differently and create businesses where economic growth and sustainability are each other's prereq-uisites and where consumption and liveability don't have to come at the expense of the environment.

We are honoured that you have chosen to join us on a transformative journey for our society and planet. A journey towards merging busi-ness and sustainability. A journey we believe strongly in with both heart and mind. We hope to show that change does not have to be a bad thing – on the contrary it can bring about increased sustainabili-ty, liveability and social cohesion.

OUR STORY

Lendager Group was built to generate positive change. Nothing more, nothing less. We believe the best way to spark this change at scale is to lead by example and make the case for regenerative business. Indeed, it is possible for business and the planet to do this together, as partners, making sure that sustainability increases the core value and serves as a strategic growth-driver, rather than just as an add-on.

We believe the way forward is to utilise our resources much better than we presently do in our linear economy. That is why we consider our main competitor to be the world's landfills and waste-incineration plants. We are probably not the type of competitor the management of such plants had seen coming just a few years ago. And we probably hadn't seen it coming either back when we started up as an architectural firm. Nevertheless, in the transition to this new paradigm of circularity, a story like ours will become more and more common. To us, it relates to the value we deliver as well as a very strong **why**. As in, "Why does Lendager Group exist and what vision guides our choices?"

Soon after Anders Lendager founded the studio in 2011, he realised that in order to create change, you must step out of your professional comfort zone and venture towards new parts of the value chain. That is how our transformation began. In the last couple of years Lendager Group has experienced tremendous growth, going from being a small architectural firm to a rapidly expanding award-winning nexus organisation. Today we are made up of three different entities: an architectural office working towards making regenerative buildings and cities, a material-production division sourcing waste materials to be up-cycled and used in new buildings, and a a strategy and innovation hub, Lendager TCW, helping business across industries to innovate and benefit from doing good by turning waste into wealth.

Lately we have been seeing how both private companies and politicians have become aware of the huge potential stored in the

circular economy and of the benefits sustainable business can provide for corporations, society and environment at the same time.
Yet, the distance between budding ideas on the one hand, and real,
large-scale action on the other can often seem unbridgeable.

This is exactly why – after a long partnership – we decided to join
forces and establish Lendager TCW. To offer visionary but hands-
on consulting that unites thought and action by generating profit
on the bottom line of our three divisions – thus proving that profit
and environmental responsibility are prerequisites for each other
– not opposites.

DITTE'S JOURNEY

In my everyday life I find myself wearing many different hats. But my preferred role is change agent, striving to secure the betterment and well-being of our society. It's always been like that. And that is exactly what this book is about. Enabling change on a global scale.

That is also why the merger with Anders and Lendager Group has been so meaningful to me. First, Lendager Group stands out as a great example of the kind of business I am convinced will play a key role in mitigating climate change. It links innovation with industry knowledge and has impact on a large commercial scale. Second, as an entrepreneur, I believe strongly in combining the traditional role of consultancy with the tangible opportunities provided by innovation. Especially for circular economy, where, despite the numerous reports and research, the full potential for viable business has yet to be fully explained. Thus, as consultants, the Lendager TCW team moves beyond deliverables within the world of Microsoft Office (Keynote, or whatever text format you use) and get our hands dirty and start producing actual on-the-ground results and implementation.

I believe change happens best when we are optimistic. So, I have chosen to be an optimist, and I work hard to maintain that perspective for myself and my team. I've created a life where I get to meet and work with talented and ambitious people who are doing everything possible to make change happen on a daily basis. In a world where an almost-constant stream of facts alerts us to the challenges we face as a global population, remaining positive is a valuable trait.

Why? Because it enables me to see things differently. To see opportunity and to act upon it.

> – To see that if we combine our global experiences across industries, harness the possibilities brought by tech, and combine it with the intelligence of nature, great opportunity arise.

So for me that is a key purpose. Utilising the fact that I get to travel and meet fantastic changemakers from all over the world. That I get to see exciting things happening anywhere; from Brazil and Columbia to Palo Alto, Scotland, Copenhagen and everything in between, to bridge across geographies and industries. Because together we can change things for the better.

To put my story as changemaker in a context, I was born and raised with the amazing privilege of being financially safe and sound. A pretty nice feeling, obviously, but it has also given me a sense of responsibility to use that opportunity and privilege to have a positive impact on the world.

I began my journey as an investor, with a particular interest in the circular economy, in my mid-twenties. At that point, I must admit, I did not know much about investing and markets. Yet, I knew instinctively that I had to make my financial decisions in my own way and make my money do more than just show a good return on a balance sheet.

So, when my family and I invested in VIGGA, a circular-economy -based baby-clothing brand – where you subscribe to the service of babywear as opposed to buying each piece of individual clothing yourself – I took a seat on the board. What compelled me to invest my time and capital in VIGGA was the positive correlation I saw between financial profit and environmental concern. The more times the clot-hes could be circulated, the better for climate health and business.

I set up an advisory board for VIGGA, and it did not take me long to ask the Danish MP Ida Auken to join. I had volunteered in strategic communications and PR during the national election in 2011, after which Ida was appointed Secretary of Environment. It became clear that we had a common interest in accelerating Denmark's transition to a circular economy, and together we founded the Danish Circular Economy Network.

It quickly became apparent to me that I wanted to dedicate both my time and portfolio to circular economy, helping to ensure a prosperous world in which all of us can thrive. So I decided to quit my day job and went back to school at the University of Cambridge. There, I delved into the wonders and horrors of sustainability and climate change in order to gain more knowledge.

Not long after came new opportunities which led me to found the consultancy The Circular Way, where I got the chance to help companies use circular economy to increase their value and competitive edge while also benefiting people and the planet.

I cannot recommend highly enough that – if you have the means and opportunity – you embark on an adventure towards sustainability for all. Sooner rather than later. The world surely needs it, and perhaps you need it as well. While the return on an investment can be calculated in financial terms, there is no way to measure the intangible rewards. In my own particular case, I think that my journey as an entrepreneur, investor and environmentalist has enabled me to be an optimist. I am increasingly positive about creating innovative strategies, helping to change the traditional ways of producing and consuming based on circularity, and making it feasible to imagine that business and the environment can be friends, not foes.

More than anything, I hope this book will enable you to stay optimistic and empower you to create change.

ANDERS' JOURNEY

My name is Anders. I am an architect and the founder of Lendager Group.

Not too long ago, I made the conscious choice of going from being a traditional architect to stepping out of my comfort zone and creating Lendager Group – an innovative nexus organisation. Here, we not only *draw* buildings. We also *produce* upcycled building materials and *help* cities and businesses to strategise on how to create sustainability. Along with my team I have made the conscious choice of always looking for the resources that are already available when we start designing new projects. This comes both with opportunity and responsibility. Because as architects we can have tremendous impact on people's lives and on society in general. We have the opportunity to make our planet better, but if we make bad choices we risk making it worse. As architects, we hold the risk and liability of the well-being of large amounts of people when we are at work. As such, we can and should also play a crucial role in creating a green, prosperous world for all to thrive in.

> – I have chosen to dedicate my life to realising that opportunity as an architect, as an employer, and as a changemaker in the built environment and society at large.

For me, that choice was already evident when I chose to apply for the architectural school. Approaching the opportunity to work with all the resources we have available around us, everywhere, discharged. To use them to create something better. Without initially knowing exactly what it meant, it was still a conscious choice – partly formed by my upbringing, now that I think of it.

My parents were children during the Second World War and grew up with a typical post-war mentality of moderation, hard work and economic frugality. And even though my mom was a banker/housewife, and my dad did banking as well as stockbroking and real estate, we never lived a life of extravagance. Au contraire. We never travelled abroad, only drove old cars, my mom used to bike throughout the city to find the best discounts, and my dad would repair everything – our bikes, the roof, the stove, our tv and even broken furniture. Nothing was thrown out as garbage, and everything we bought as new was more than well-considered. To say the least. I was always annoyed as a child for not having the newest technology, a new bike or a car of a good brand. But that was only until I turned 8 or 9 and started imitating my dad, finding joy in making new stuff out of waste. Like the time when I found some old, red Jaguar car seats and made them into a couch and some armchairs attached to the old car tires. Or as when my older brother taught me how to weld when I was maybe 10 or 11, and old bikes suddenly became home-made but functional scooters after a few adjustments. It was a time with very few restrictions, where I was allowed and encouraged to carry out my very first experiments with upcycling waste materials.

A school project that really made a change for me was when I took an internship in Los Angeles. Working on a luxury villa for an entrepreneur with a strange passion for trucks. The design of his new house had already been going on for many years when I joined. One part of the project was to create a concrete lap swimming pool facing a beautiful view of downtown Los Angeles. But looking at the resources available I got an idea: What if we used one of his trucks to create the lap pool instead?

That would save loads of resources and CO_2-emissions – while at the same time also giving him the chance to use on of his dearly beloved trucks every day when swimming his round of laps. We installed it in such a way that it went straight through the facade from outdoors and directly into his bedroom. Imagine waking up in the morning. Jumping straight into your pool – created with and reminding you of your great passion – while looking out at the city that made you.

He loved it. And later I realised that the reason why he loved it was because of the completed narrative he got of his house. Connecting the architecture and the city of Los Angeles physically to his own career, legacy and passion for trucks. In total, the project created a solution that brought an unutilised resource back into function – saving the environment a great amount of CO_2-emissions – while at the same time giving the client an additional aesthetic and sentimental value.

What I want you to get from this story are two things.

First. At that time, I did not know about circular economy, let alone the concept of cradle2cradle, and I was not doing it with a sustainability perspective at all. I did it because it made sense to me as an architect, and similarly you will make choices that makes sense to you too. Choices that your gut tells you are the right ones. And when looking back, years later, you will realise why you did as you did – and learn new things from your own choices and your own actions.

Secondly, I want to make sure you are aware of the importance in creating a narrative around what we do as architects. Because if we are to succeed at creating a better world for all to thrive in, it is crucial that we make sustainability relevant and comprehensible for everybody. That we communicate – loud and clear – how and why it is important for each and every one of us.

For me, the internship in Los Angeles made the difference. Getting a network and an understanding of that type of architecture on the US west coast. It gave me scares and opportunities – both of which have shaped my path and understanding of architecture. Learnings I would not be without. You will find similar situations. So, my advice to you is: *make sure they are based on conscious choices – not just pure coincidence*s. Choose what you want, what you believe in.

A few years after school I choose to start first Lendager Architects and then Lendager Group as a rebellion against the traditional industry and as an opportunity to do things differently. Luckily, I now know that I made the right choice. The industry is moving and change is coming. The future of architecture is to change the world for the better. Now, I hope you will join me and the many architects around the world, that are working around the clock to make that a reality, sooner than later.

A CHANGEMAKER'S GUIDE

In *Part I*, we present our case to you. WHY we have to do things differently, and WHY we believe circular economy is the right way to do so. We tell you about the global potential of shifting towards circularity and let you in on our grand vision - showing you how far we can actually go 'simply' by changing our existing mind-set.

In *Part II*, we take a closer look at the role of design in the transition to a circular economy. We argue that design-thinking is the starting point and that changing our perception of waste plays a crucial role in this process. We present our manifesto of designing for circularity and highlight our own experiences of upcycling waste materials in two cases from the built environment. Lastly, we give you our interpretation of H.C. Andersen's classical fairytale of Blockhead Hans as seen from a circular economy point of view.

In Part III, we zoom in on the role of cities and look at how they can play a crucial part in the transformation toward a global regenerative society. We go through the changing roles and understandings of the city in a historical context and give examples of how the future city is going to operate in connection to its buildings and citizens. We then present a new science of cities by combining urban metabolism and circular economy in making the city a regenerative unit that offers the solutions to our SDGs from various but related angles.

In *Part IV*, we create a roadmap for positive change by going into detail with the important role of business. We explain how cross -sector partnerships, new technological breakthroughs, the re-creation of our value chains and the implementation of completely new business models can make true sustainability evident and viable – benefitting both people, profit and planet. Doing so, we are hopeful of giving you a solid starting point for enabling change yourself. Whether it is as a changemaker on the individual level, as a business professional, or at an industry, city or societal level. We guide you on where and how to start – and offer you an insight on our chosen methodology.

Why

"We cannot predict the future, but we can invent it"

Nobel Prize winner Dennis Gabor, 1963

CHANGE THE RULES
OF THE GAME

"You can't build the business of tomorrow on the
network of yesterday."

The quote comes from an advertisement in *Fast Company* – a
monthly magazine[1] and go-to point for global news on disruption
and futurist thinking. We couldn't agree more with this message.
But, while the ad speaks only of the Internet and digital networks,
we believe it relates just as much to our overall society and economic
structures. The current world economy is the economy of yesterday,
and only with a new structure can we ensure a more liveable, feasible and dynamic tomorrow.

1. March 2017 issue

Why so? In order to truly enable sustainable innovations and be
certain they succeed on a large scale, we have to change the rules
of the game. It cannot be a zero-sum competition, where there
must be losers in order to have winners. Especially in terms of the
current mind-set that believes investing in business and the environment is an either/or choice. Instead, we must create a win-win
game for the environment, businesses, and everyone who chooses
to participate in the new paradigm. Where growth and value are
decoupled from emissions and the use of virgin materials.

In short, we see three types of businesses: those that are built
with sustainability as their core; those that understand they need
to transform toward sustainability; and those whose businesses
are built on "stranded assets", in which a fundamental reboot
of their investments is necessary if they themselves are not to
become stranded.

Will there be pushback? Definitely. Because as Thomas Kuhn put
it in *The Structure of Scientific Revolutions*[2]: "A known predeces-
sor to a paradigm shift is a pronounced and undefined anxiety
by those participating in the current paradigm." Kuhn is correct,
because – let's be honest – companies that keep burning fuel
and produce endless amounts of waste will fail. But only because

2. Written in 1962, "The
Structure of Scientific
Revolutions" is a book
on philosophy of science
in which Thomas Kuhn
introduces the notion of
a paradigm shift for the
first time.

they choose not to accept the new paradigm, where sustainability and a good bottom-line are mutually beneficial prerequisites – not opposites or enemies.

And, yes, putting a price on negative environmental externalities definitely plays a role here, but only because it enables the solution. It is not the solution itself. Righting wrongs and ensuring a fair market structure might be crucial to the success of innovations. But to ensure a positive outcome, we must fundamentally change the game and start valuing our resources for what they really are.

How? By opening our eyes and making sure that "doing good" for the environment equals doing better business. From where we stand, business should be the driving force of transformation by creating innovations that translate visionary ideas into tangible value.

WITH BOTH EYES OPEN

Having "both eyes open" is a notion we got from Bill Gates. After the COP21 in 2015 - the UN's climate change conference - Gates wrote a blog[3] based on the book Sustainable Materials: With Both Eyes Open, written by a brilliant team of Cambridge University scientists. The team's research project had made Gates aware that we need to change the way we use materials and that our current business model of "doing less bad'" usually means having only one eye open and the other closed. The point is, that "less bad" is not enough. It narrows your vision and leaves you in a vulnerable position; making you easily disrupted and overtaken. So how do we operate with both eyes open?

3. Gates Notes, 2015.
Reduce; Reuse; Retool

According to Gates, part of the answer lies in "studying how you could use less material to begin with, make products that last longer, reuse or recycle them, or avoid using the service the material provides." In other words, start designing our materials, products and business models for circularity. Only in this way can we realise the full potential of our opportunities, mitigate climate change and create a regenerative society. If you want to know more about Bill Gates's eureka moment, the Cambridge research group, led by Julian Allwood and Jonathan Cullen, have made their book and all their research available online [4].

4. Read more on:
www.withbotheyesopen.com

That the eyes with which we view our opportunities and constraints matter is nothing new. We seek creative ideas from a broad spectrum of thinkers. From Immanuel Kant, whose doctrine of transcendental idealism[5] on how our personal perspective (what Kant describes as the colour of tint of our glasses) creates the way we see the external world and structure our experience, to our personal hero Alexander Von Humboldt[6], who described the ability to see things differently when we free ourselves from existing structures. Or as his brother and fellow philosopher Wilhelm von Humboldt put it: "If we glance at the most important revolutions in history, we see at once that the greatest number of these originated in the periodical revolutions of the human mind."[7]

Thus, we need to raise our level of ambition from "less bad" to "actual good" or even "excellent". This is true not just because extending ourselves to our uttermost and reaching our full potential give us a competitive advantage in our individual businesses, but also because the world, as a global community, needs our best efforts to reduce climate change.

5. This concept was first described in Kant's book "The critique of pure reason" from 1781.

6. (1769-1859) - A nature scientist and explorer best known for his travels in Latin America and his substantial work on botanical geography.

7. This quote comes from the book "The limits of state action" from 1792, a philosophical essay considered a great work of the German Age of Enlightenment.

Photo of Anders Lendager from our HAL 9000-like presentation video of the Wasteland Exhibition.

This shift in perspective is the reason why we chose "2001: A Space Odyssey" as our reference point when Lendager Group created the exhibition "Wasteland"[8] at the Danish Architecture Centre in Copenhagen. We constructed a monolith of upcycled concrete outside the entrance to the exhibition and demonstrated the potential of building tomorrow with the waste of today. We wanted to give the visitors the opportunity to touch this "structure," as a physical representation of the opening of a new world order, a new paradigm. Just as in Stanley Kubrick's film, where the monolith symbolises the beginning of evolution.

8. Wasteland - from waste to architecture was first launched in 2017 with the purpose of displaying selected projects in which architectural concepts help solve some of the global challenges facing the world.

Similarly, the exhibition uses a *HAL 9000*-like video of Anders Lendager to emphasise that change is coming and that it is time to join the journey towards the future.

What we see is a need to merge different schools of thoughts, notions and ways of doing, fundamentally moving away from a linear pattern of production and consumption while still celebrating three core drivers: innovation, catering to global demand, and growing our businesses. We believe that, if we open both our eyes and combine these three skills, we can make the transition to a regenerative economy enabled by a circular economy.

INNOVATION AND GROWTH
THE CIRCULAR WAY

Consumption and growth enable the financial opportunity to change our current ways of doing and enable future solutions. However innovation is the key to unlocking the opportunity for us to start producing and consuming in a fundamentally different way – a circular way.

While we are aware that we need to do a lot of things differently, we also recognise that as humans we have already made incredible progress. We have built great cities and developed technological solutions that have brought innovation, prosperity and opportunities.

Take deep water drilling as an example. Despite us now being fully aware of its harmful impact on the planet[9], it is nonetheless an example of great innovation and technological development. And while deep water drilling should be relegated to our past, the skills and experience we gained are still relevant today. Going forward, instead of simply shying away from all the great skills and experience of our predecessors – many of which are still relevant today – we must build upon the power of industrialisation – but *the circular way*.

Circular economy is a fundamentally new way of looking at resources, a way that enables us to uncouple growth from the use of new resources and materials by extending the life-cycle

9. In 2010, Deepwater horizon - an ultra-deepwater offshore drilling rig located in the Gulf of Mexico - exploded. Killing 11 crew-members and resulting in the biggest maritime oil spill in history.

of existing resources – either by keeping them in their first use or by bringing them back into circulation in a new way[10]. The latter is not a fancy word for recycling – recycling is just one sub-element within the circular economy.

So when we talk about circular economy, we are referring to the idea of seeing and using resources according to their true value instead of throwing them away as waste. There are four crucial reasons why we believe so strongly in circular economy.

10. The notion of a circular economy most likely dates back to 1966, where the American economist Kenneth E. Boulding described the contrast between an "open economy" with infinite input and a "closed economy" where a certain amount of input "remain forever a part of the concerns of the economy".

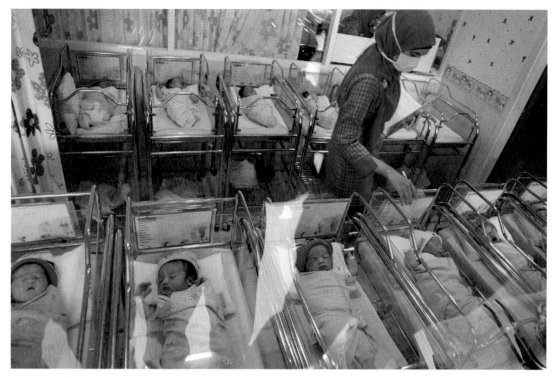

A nurse at the Mother and Child Hospital in Surabaya in East Java Province looks after 13 newborn babies born on December 12, 2012 (Ritzau Scanpix/Juni Kriswanto)

1.   BIRTH:
The increase in births and the growth of the middle class

First, the rapid rise of the global population and of a strong middle class in the developing world create prosperity but also an enormous surge in demand and consumption. By the end of 2050, the world population is projected to be 9.8 billion[11] people, and the global middle class is set to grow by 160 million[12] each year for the next 10 years at least. As a result, over the next 30 years, the global demand for housing, goods, energy and transportation will skyrocket.

11. UN Department of Economic and Social Affairs, 2017. World Population Prospects; The 2017 Revision
12. Kharas, H., 2017. The unprecedented expansion of the global middle class: an update

A house in Union Beach, New Jersey, half washed away by the Hurricane Sandy in 2012.
(Ritzau Scanpix/Dennis Van Tine)

2.   DECAY:
More natural catastrophes

Second, climate change is already taking place, and at a rapid pace that is. This is causing an increase in natural catastrophes all over the world in various forms; cloudbursts, hurricanes, floods, droughts, wildfire and famines. The world is in decay; destroying buildings, cities, crops, forests, coral reefs and animal species. Without real climate change mitigation, more than 140 million people could be on the run as climate refugees by the year of 2050[13].

13. The World Bank, 2018. Groundswell: Preparing for Internal Climate Migration

Thich Quang Duc, a Buddhist monk, burns himself to death on a Saigon street June 11, 1963 to protest alleged persecution of Buddhists by the South Vietnamese government. (AP Photo/Malcolm Browne)

3. MODERATION:
The need to avoid temperature rise above 1.5° celsius[14]

Third, to avoid the worst case scenario of climate change, we must lower our carbon footprint radically. If the not, the world as we know it today will change for good. Disconcertingly, global emissions of greenhouse gases are currently rising still. According to the UN Intergovernmental Panel on Climate Change (IPCC) emissions should be lowered by 40% to 70% (compared to 2010) by 2050 if we are to succeed in lowering emissions to an acceptable level[15].

14. United Nations, 2015. Adoptions of the Paris Agreement
15. IPCC, 2014. Climate Change 2014: Synthesis Report

Father and son on a storyfoam boat collecting plastic bottles they can sell in junkshops in Manila on March 19, 2015. (Ritzau Scanpix/Noel Celis)

4.   SALVATION:
An abundance of waste

Last but not least, we have too much waste. The oceans are filled with plastic; beaches are piled up with landfill waste; and we continuously throw out so much that global waste management can barely keep up.

Based on these four facts, the global challenge might seem huge and the consequences frightening, but they also offer an opportunity for businesses to be part of the solution by satisfying growing demands without harming our environment. Above all, the situation requires us to start producing and consuming resources and goods in a fundamentally different way – a circular way.

A CLOSER LOOK AT
THE CIRCULAR ECONOMY

The current abundance of waste, the growing population and the rising demand for goods don't necessarily have to impact our climate negatively. Instead of focusing on waste management, we can start looking to designers, resource brokers, architects and others to transform a waste-and-demand problem into a solution that involves making our abundant resources ready for their second, third or maybe tenth time of reuse.

HOW CAN THE CIRCULAR ECONOMY
MAKE BUSINESS AND SUSTAINABILITY ALLIES
AND NOT ENEMIES?

In order to seize the full potential of a material, either the material itself or the product must be designed to create value through circulation. Take, for instance, the efforts of the company Caterpillar which has been introducing remanufacturing and rebuildings programs - keeping resources in their value chain through a circular flow of materials. This allows for lower-cost products and great service options. Using a similar approach, at Schiphol Airport in Amsterdam, Philips is moving towards a circular product-as-a-service business model by offering lighting as a service provider rather than as a seller of lamps or light bulbs as a product. Does that distinction really change the situation? You might ask that question – because, regardless of what Philips sells (or does not sell) in the airport, it is still installing lamps, which still use light bulbs. However, the result represents a fundamental shift of the business incentives. According to the old logic; the bigger the sales, the bigger the growth and the better the business. But by adopting a service-business model, Philips has changed the rules of the game. Now, the longer a product lasts and the better its quality, the better the business and the less the negative environmental impact. In this way, good business and a healthy planet are interdependent.

BIOLOGICAL CYCLES

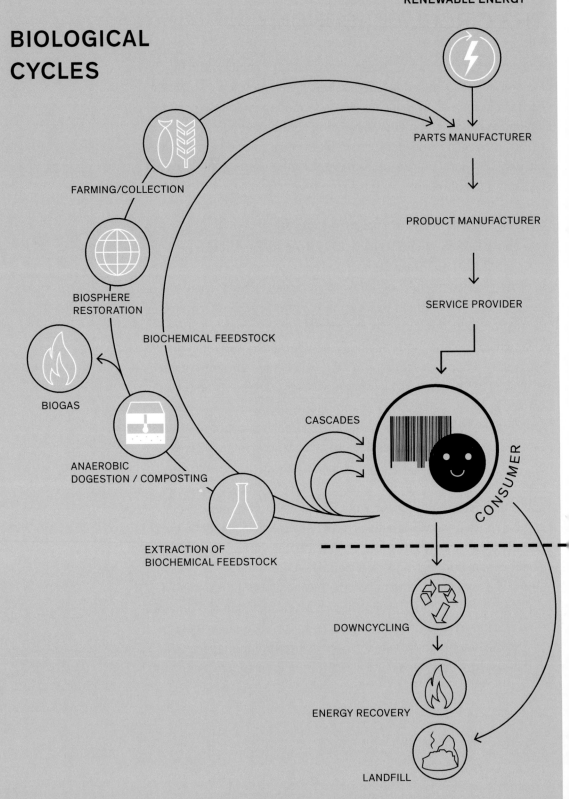

INCREASINGLY POWERED BY RENEWABLE ENERGY

PARTS MANUFACTURER

PRODUCT MANUFACTURER

SERVICE PROVIDER

CONSUMER

FARMING/COLLECTION

BIOSPHERE RESTORATION

BIOCHEMICAL FEEDSTOCK

BIOGAS

ANAEROBIC DOGESTION / COMPOSTING

CASCADES

EXTRACTION OF BIOCHEMICAL FEEDSTOCK

DOWNCYCLING

ENERGY RECOVERY

LANDFILL

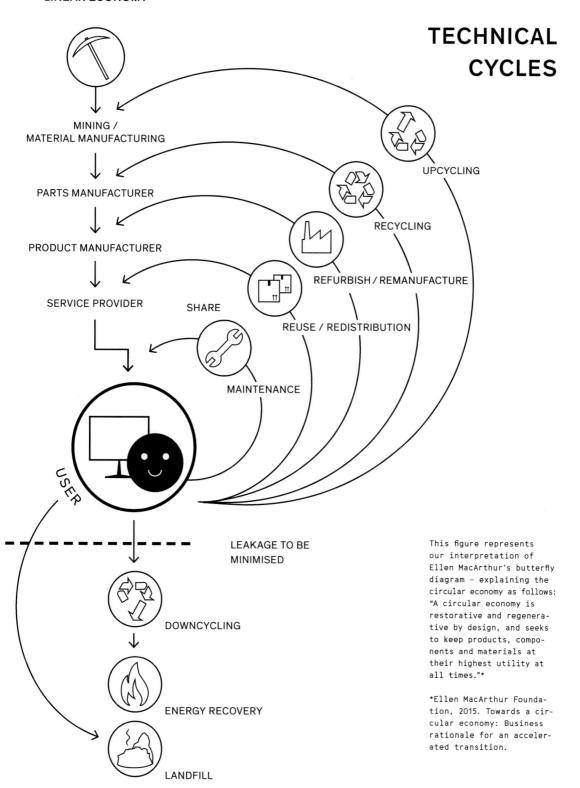

**TRADITIONAL
LINEAR ECONOMY**

TECHNICAL CYCLES

MINING /
MATERIAL MANUFACTURING

UPCYCLING

PARTS MANUFACTURER

RECYCLING

PRODUCT MANUFACTURER

REFURBISH / REMANUFACTURE

SERVICE PROVIDER

SHARE

REUSE / REDISTRIBUTION

MAINTENANCE

USER

LEAKAGE TO BE
MINIMISED

DOWNCYCLING

ENERGY RECOVERY

LANDFILL

This figure represents our interpretation of Ellen MacArthur's butterfly diagram – explaining the circular economy as follows: "A circular economy is restorative and regenerative by design, and seeks to keep products, components and materials at their highest utility at all times."*

*Ellen MacArthur Foundation, 2015. Towards a circular economy: Business rationale for an accelerated transition.

Figure 02: Cascading of Materials

MATERIAL USE, INCLUDING:
BRICKS, CONCRETE, WOOD, GLASS, PLASTIC, STEEL
LANDFILL
ENERGY RECOVERY
LOW
VALUE
HIGH
UPCYCLING
DOWNCYCLING
THE CHOICE IS YOURS

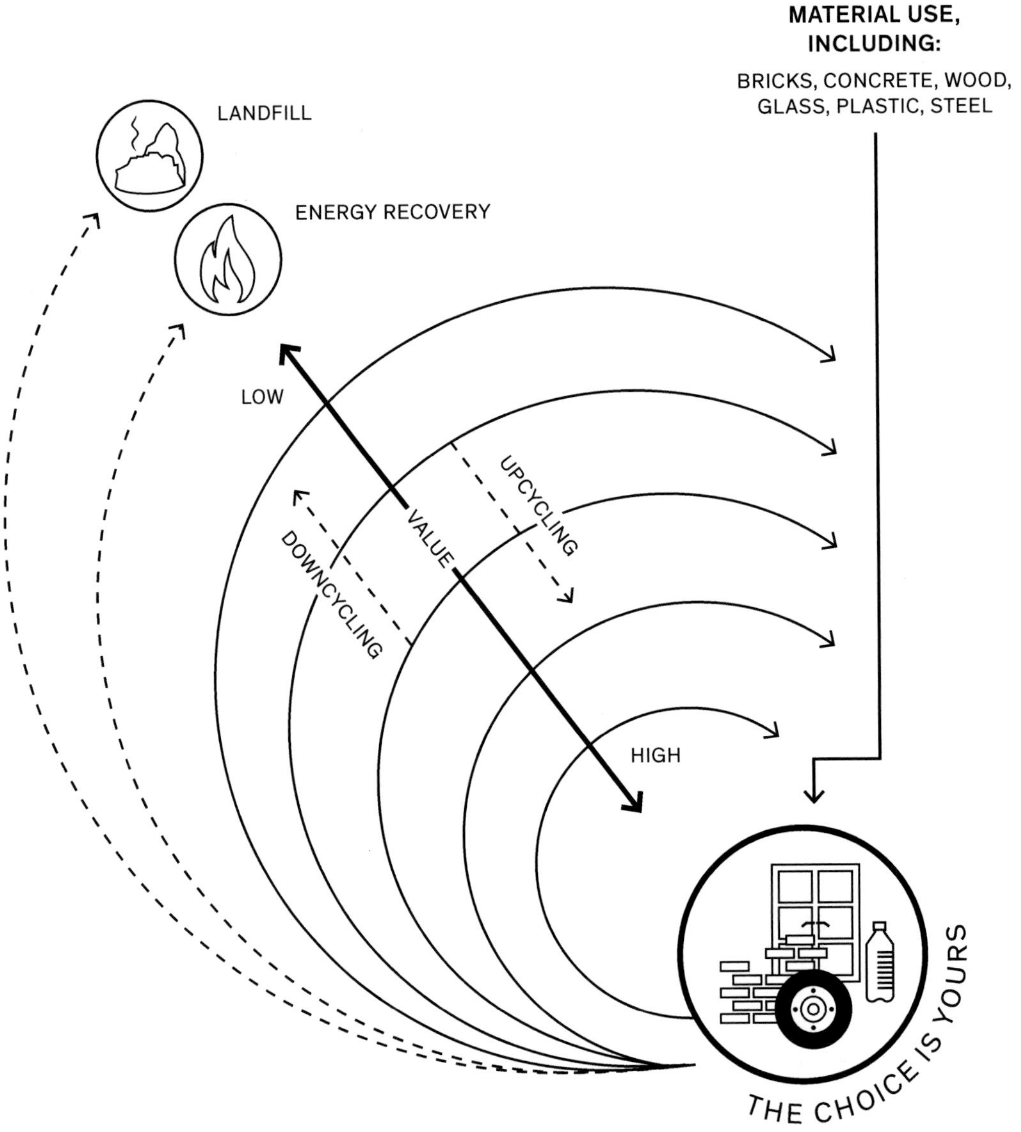

Cascading represents the idea of prolonging a material's life and value for as long or as many times as possible. To exploit the inherent potential and value in any material, before we let it go to waste. Energy recovery should always be the last resort.

GLOSSARY

CIRCULAR ECONOMY
An economic system where value is decoupled from virgin resources.

RETHINK
To rethink our behavior. The way we design, produce, work and consume, increasing availability, reusability and recoverability.

REDUCE
To use less – either in production or in consumption.

REPAIR
To fix a faulty material or product – bringing it back to functionality.

REUSE
To use a material or product again directly without breaking it down or changing it; by re-selling, sharing, leasing etc.

REMANUFACTURE
To restore or reconfigure a product from a mix of used, repaired and new parts – performing on par with a "new" product.

RECYCLE
To recover a material while keeping its original value or purpose.

UPCYCLE
To recover or reuse a waste material by making it a new resource. Using innovation to create a product that outperforms a benchmark in terms of quality, CO_2 and aesthetics.

DOWNCYCLE
To recover or reuse a waste material by making it a new resource, but at a lower value than originally.

ENERGY RECOVERY
To treat waste by converting materials into energy in the form of electricity, heat or fuel.

LANDFILLING
To dispose waste materials at a designated land site.

RESSOURCE INNOVATION
The process of inventing new methods of circulating materials and products.

DESIGN FOR DISASSEMBLY
To design objects from parts and materials that can easily be taken apart after usage and either reused or recycled.

WASTE
A discarded material or product not fulfilling its potential value and function. In other words: an untapped resource.

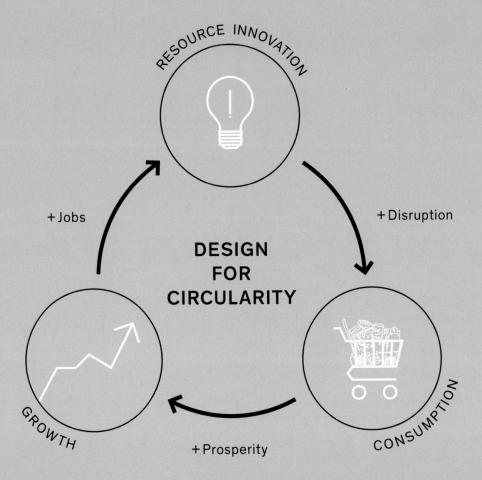

RESOURCE INNOVATION

+Jobs

+Disruption

**DESIGN
FOR
CIRCULARITY**

GROWTH

CONSUMPTION

+Prosperity

One more example can be found in VIGGA, a Danish baby-clothing brand, which was Ditte's first venture into circular economy back in 2014. The founders of the company had previously had a different baby-clothing brand whose goal was do things as sustainably as possible in terms of, for example, material choices. Eventually, however, they came to realise the following: As long as they were operating within the existing, linear structures of a take-make-dispose economy, their financial performance was based on the economic principle, "the more you sell (and, thus, have to produce) the more money you earn," rather than making a positive difference on the environment. So back in 2014 they decided to shift gears. They founded VIGGA as a product-as-a-service business, where customers do not buy baby clothes. Instead, they have a monthly subscription, which ensures that the babies always have a great-looking garment in the right size. After one consumer has used the clothes, the company takes it back and checks and cleans it before it is recirculated to the next subscribing user.

As Vigga Svensson, VIGGA co-founder and CEO says,

> "It has always been extremely important for us
> to act sustainably. By designing our business
> model and our product for circularity, we had the
> tool-set to change our business from doing 'less
> bad' to actually doing 'good.'"

All of a sudden, high-quality clothing and long product life are the keys to financial performance. The better the quality of the material and design, the more times the individual piece can be circulated — and every circulation improves the bottom line.

We think VIGGA as well as the Philips and Catapiller examples highlight the difference between a circular-based business model and a traditional linear one that involves take-make-dispose. It also shows how designing for circularity is different from designing for classical reuse. Why? Because having a vision as well as a financial incentive to create attractive clothes that are also long-lasting meant adding a unique design phase of creating and testing colours, materials, and styles.

As we see it, it's this simple: If you design your businesses, cities, products and materials so that resources stay in circulation, you and your stakeholders will gain the greatest possible value out of a minimal amount of material and thereby reduce harmful emissions. What's not to like?

That is why a circular economy differs from many of the traditional concepts about sustainability on a global level: Limited resources make for limited competition. As we will clarify in *Part II*, Designing for prosperity, we see it differently. Instead of accepting scarcity as a given, we maintain that we have all the resources we need. Our thesis is not that the resources themselves are finite – what is limited is our failure to see, use and value these assets, which we now disregard as waste.

In making this argument, we see a unique opportunity to design the future we need to ensure sustainable, affordable products without compromising on cost, quality or aesthetics. This enables us to mitigate climate change while catering to the rising global demand by decoupling growth from material consumption – and earning a profit while doing so.

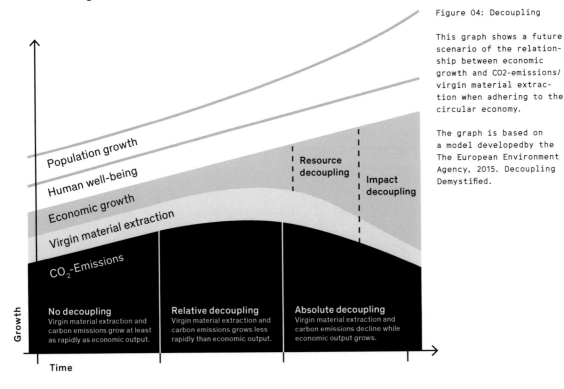

Figure 04: Decoupling

This graph shows a future scenario of the relationship between economic growth and CO2-emissions/virgin material extraction when adhering to the circular economy.

The graph is based on a model developedby the The European Environment Agency, 2015. Decoupling Demystified.

"Circular economy is the opportunity of a lifetime to create sustainable business benefitting both people, planet and profit. Luckily more and more business leaders are realising it, and it has been great to see that since we first started pushing the agenda through The Young Global Leaders programme, the rest of Davos has now caught up, and circular economy is now one of hottest topics in Davos"

Ida Auken, World Economic Forum CE META COUNCIL co-chair
& WEF YOUNG GLOBAL LEADER

THE WINNING HAND

Even though the circular economy helps us solve many of the global challenges outlined at the COP21 in Paris and in the initiative of the United Nations' Sustainable Development Goals (SDGs), saving the planet is not our only concern. If we succeed in innovating and in transforming our economy to be circular—and, thus, scalable—tremendous economic gains could follow[16]. But, for this to be the case, we must raise our level of ambition and reach for the stars, creating businesses and services that put sustainability at their core (not as an add on), whose carbon footprint will only get smaller as the business grows. The better the business, the bigger the impact. That fact accounts for the continuously increasing interest in circular economy at the annual World Economic Forum in Davos:

*UPCYCLE HOUSE
Type: Residential
Area: 140 square metres
Site: Nyborg, Denmark
Construction budget:
1.7 mio. kr.
Client: Realdania
By & Byg
Partners: Egen Vinding
og Datter and MOE A/S
Architect: Lendager ARC
Status: Build
Year: 2011 - 2013
Partner in charge:
Anders Lendager
Project leader:
Anders Lendager
Team: Rune Sjöstedt Sode,
Christoffer Carlsen,
Jenny Haraldsdottir,
Anna Zobel

But it isn't easy. We need to revise our consumption and production patterns drastically-giving up the linear economy paradigm for good and adopting a system where resources and products are put into circulation rather than thrown out and wasted. Imagine, for example, building a house our of champagne corks, old newspapers and other recycled products. It sounds strange, if not impossible. Nevertheless, commissioned by Realdania in the Danish town of Nyborg, we made such a house* entirely out of consumer waste without compromising aesthetics, profit or quality.

In fact, the possibilities of transitioning to a circular economy are too many to list here. An analysis by the Ellen MacArthur Foundation and McKinsey & Company suggests that by minimising the use of non-sustainable materials in consumer goods, we can save $700 billion globally[17]. As we hope to show in this book, with the right blend of ambition, and industry know-how, plus the refusal to accept obstacles, we can create step-by-step, practical solutions.

"I am putting myself to the fullest possible use, which is all I think any conscious entity can ever hope to do." - HAL 9000[18].

16. In a fact sheet "Circular economy – closing the loop" from the European Commission in 2015, they point out that by the year of 2030, the transition to circular economy could lead to "Savings of €600 billion for EU businesses, equivalent to 8% of their annual turnover, creation of 580,000 jobs and the reduction of EU carbon emissions by 450 million tonnes."

17. Ellen MacArthur Foundation, 2015. Delivering the circular economy: A toolkit for policymakers

18. 2001: A Space Odyssey (1968)

THE COURTYARD
OF THE FUTURE

On July 2, 2011, the clouds burst over the Copenhagen metropolitan area. 135 millimetres of rain and more than 5000 lightning strikes hit the city in less than 3 hours. The result: heat and power cuts, flooding, severely damaged buildings, burn injuries, pollution, increased risk of infections, IT-breakdowns, overheated phone-lines, patient evacuation from hospitals and a collapsed infrastructure. In the end, more than 90.000 claims of water-damage were reported, passing on a massive bill of almost $1 billion in total (6.2 billion DKK) to the insurance companies[19]. That day, Copenhagen experienced the most expensive cloudburst in Europe's history[20].

The Courtyard of the Future is a much-needed reinvention of the outdoor space nestled among urban building blocks in the cities – open to the sky and full of potential. Developed on Straussvej in Copenhagen – in close collaboration with the local residents and Copenhagen municipality's urban renewal team – the Courtyard of the future offers an innovative solution to several challenges, most importantly: **flash flooding**. Not just to Copenhagen but to all metropolitan areas in the world.

itation in large parts of central and northern Europe (of up to about 30 %) and a decrease in southern Europe (of up to 40 %) from 1971–2000 to 2071–2100. More flooding in the north, more drought in the south[21].

19. The City of Copenhagen: Cloudburst Management Plan 2012

20. Munch, S., 2012. Historisk skybrud blev Europas dyreste. Jyllands-Posten

21. Smiatek, G. et al, 2016. EURO-CORDEX regional climate model analysis for the Greater Alpine Region: Performance and expected future change

Because right now, global warming is causing more extreme weather conditions around the world and we are seeing a dramatic change in precipitation patterns, with fewer rain events, but of greater intensity. Projections indicate an increase in annual precip-

One major reason why climate change is posing such a great threat to our cities and societal wellbeing – and caused so big damages to Copenhagen in such a short time – is the lack of proper sewage systems. Inspired by the systems of Hamburg, Paris and London, the Copenhagen sewer network was laid in the 1850s. To renovate and futureproof that network in accordance with today's precipitation patterns and risks of cloudburst would cost between $3.1 to $4.7 billion[22]. And renovating/expanding the sewage system is far from enough. An extensive holistic strategy for green city planning over the next 20 years is imperative. A strategy in

which the built environment plays a vital role as part of the solution to climate mitigation. In the many courtyards of Copenhagen, a typical solution thus far has been to dig out great cloudburst-pools where excess rainwater can slowly trickle down and relieve the sewers. But doing so it a resource intensive process that in itself can be damaging the environment and will limit the usage of the courtyard for the residents quite a bit.

22. Københavns Kommune, 2015. Klimatilpasning og skybrudssikring af København

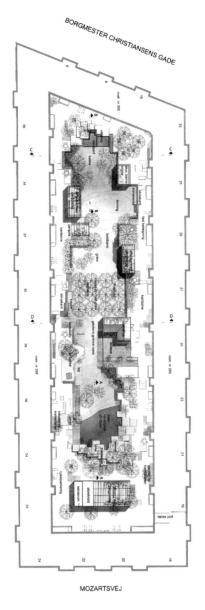

The Courtyard of the Future uses the increasing risk of cloudbursts as a valuable design element – turning problems into resources.

THE COURTYARD OF THE FUTURE
Location: Sydhavn, Copenhagen, Denmark
Area: 3250 square metres
Status: In progress. Due to be
completed in late 2018
Client: Copenhagen Municipality
Architect: Lendager Architects
Material supplier: Lendager Up
Landscape architect: BOGL
Engineer: Sloth Møller

A green oasis inside the Courtyard of the Future with vegetable patches
and recreational areas.

A green oasis inside the Courtyard of the Future with vegetable patches and recreational areas.

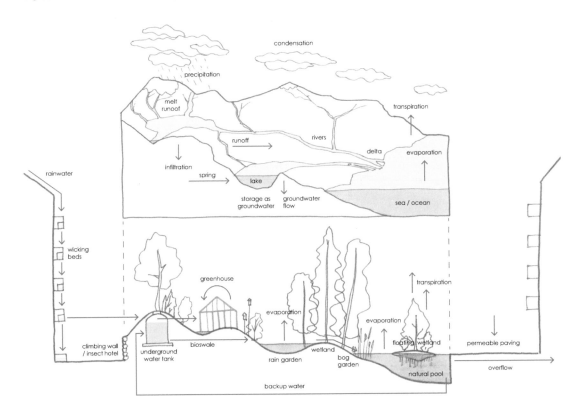

Case 1: The Courtyard of the Future

THE CLIMATE WALL
– IMITATING THE DESIGN
OF NATURE.

So, with the courtyard of the future, we wanted to reach for the stars and do it differently. Instead of digging down we found a new way to build up. A way to imitate nature's very own water cycle by designing a so-called climate wall. The climate wall is a low wall made from modular building blocks with various configurations, encircling the entire courtyard and demarking a green lake-area in the center. The building blocks are made from upcycled concrete – cost-efficient and saving the environment from large amounts of CO2-emissions.

This is how it works: The inside of the climate wall is a green oasis in different levels with enough space for ball games, hide-and-seek and snowball fights during the winter. In case of a heavy cloudburst, the rainwater circulates from the perimeter of the climate wall, going through biological cleaning filters, and into the green oasis where a pristine lake is then formed. Cleaning the water on its way to the inside of the climate wall is a strict requirement from the municipality and an important step towards turning the tables for good. To take a destructive and much-feared force and make it into an asset for the local community. The lake is thus not only a tool to prevent flooding, but equally an integrated part of the courtyard that brings new opportunities to its local residents. Creating a both fertile and valuable habitat for humans, animals and plants.

Outside the climate wall you find access to all staircases and different types of areas for daily activities. Shelters for bike parking and baby carriages. Containers for waste sorting. Pergolas, and benches, tables and chairs for garden dinners or studying. There is even a greenhouse with room for subtropical plants, wine, germination and joint events. Even though the greenhouse is unheated, its glass facades collect the sun's energy and extend the outdoor season in the courtyard with up to 100 days. Imagine what a difference that will make for the average pale Dane only used to a reasonable outdoor temperature for a just a few months annually.

The design comes from the notion of biomimicry, "an approach to innovation that seeks sustainable solutions to human challenges by emulating nature's time-tested patterns and strategies"[23]. The courtyard of the future is thus an imitation of a natural watercourse that actively plays a crucial role in the overall health of the built environment. In this case, the combination of the functions available in the courtyard makes up a strong social platform – opening up for tool-sharing and events such as local harvesting and ice-skating at different times of the year.

23. What is Biomimicry?, Biomimicry Institute, 2018.

Moreover, it is a strong demonstration of how by combining circular economy and design, we can make valuable opportunities out of hitherto grand challenges. As we stressed in the beginning, the solution was developed by including the residents into the collaboration between architects, engineers, suppliers and municipality.

A green oasis inside the Courtyard of the Future with vegetable patches and recreational areas.

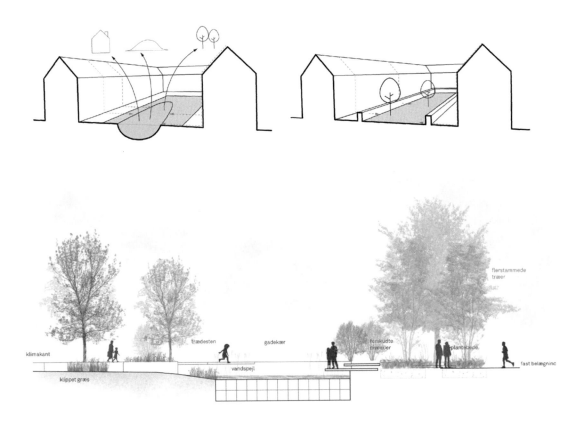

Case 1: The Courtyard of the Future   50

Comparing the traditional courtyard renovations with the courtyard of the future, the initial costs are similar – and in the long run the courtyard of the future will save us from heavy operational costs because of its natural yet adjustable design. At the end of the day, the courtyard of the future means the following four things:

1. The city and the municipality does not have to dig up streets to install increasingly large sewer infrastructure (nor do they have to dig up the courtyards).

2. In the future, a 3-hour cloudburst does not have to result in 90.000 claims and damages worth more than $1 billion.

3. The residents are gifted with high-quality recreational facilities right next to their homes.

4. And, perhaps most important of all, the Courtyard of the Future can be re-imagined and implemented on a large scale in courtyards all over the world – wherever similar climate issues pose a problem.

In the case of an extreme cloudburst, the climate wall will confine the rainwater, making sure the water does not go directly into the sewage system or into the basements of the residents.

Designing for prosperity

"A designer is an emerging synthesis of artist, inventor, mechanic, objective economist, and evolutionary strategist"

R. Buckminster Fuller – architect, author, futurist

DOES DESIGN MATTER?

The previous section was all about breaking down the imaginary wall between business and sustainability, between quality of life for our growing population and the wellbeing of Mother Earth. Magic happens when we tear down that wall and look at new business models driven by sustainable growth, making environmental and social responsibility and profit each other's prerequisites – not opposites.

But first: Why design? Why do we believe design is the essential starting point for a regenerative future? Because design is deliberate. There is an inherent value in the design process, due to the choices we actively make. A colour, an object, a specific shape –our decisions are never random but always thought through, made with both eyes open and by questioning the status quo. Therefore, to us, design is functionality. It enables intentionality. It is the act of designing that enables us to change the rules of the game in order to create a regenerative society for all to thrive in.

Right now, we often see the ideas of a "healthy environment" and of a "good business" framed as obvious contradictions – and presently for good reason. The more products we buy and consume, the more virgin materials and energy companies consume. The consequences of this process are the exhaustion of Earth's resources and a worrisome increase of CO_2-emissions. But it doesn't have to be like that. By using a design-based, circular approach to creating products, materials and business models, where value and growth are disconnected from the use of virgin materials and CO_2-emissions, we have the opportunity to change the current situation and create a new world order. An order in which economic growth is linked to respect and care for our planet and our climate.

Coming back to the initial question of Why design? The answer: Because design is the key to unlocking the potential of a prosperous world. We just need to get better at activating the potential.

Designing for circularity is not about making already existing products more effective, nor is it about developing sustainable add-ons.

Circular design is about changing our methods. We need to rethink our products and our business models. We need to completely disable the connection between the individual citizen, company and society from the consumption of virgin resources and materials. And we must do so without compromising on aesthetics, quality, economy or our environment.

Essentially, design is about
changing the world for the better.

DESIGN THE WORLD OF TOMORROW WITH THE WASTE OF TODAY

Luxurious, high-quality, handcrafted design – made of scrap from your local landfill? Doesn't exactly sound your like your traditional premium-product description, does it? Yet in the not-too-distant future it might be the norm. One of the core goals of a circular economy is to prevent waste generation and materials from ending up in a dump - in the long run making landfills obsolete. But first, we have to find new ways to make use of the immense amount of waste we have generated in the past centuries. And start by mapping and collecting the waste we have already lost track of.

In the linear economy, the amount of waste generation is generally determined by economic development, income levels and the degree of urbanisation. In 2002, 2.9 billion urban residents generated 680 million tons of municipal solid waste (MSW). Ten years later, this amount had increased to 1.3 billion tons of MSW, although the urban population only grew by 1 billion. With the urban population and global middle-class expected to increase rapidly over the next decades, the global generation of MSW is expected to about double by 2025 – meaning that, by then, 4.3 billion urban residents could be accumulating 2.2 billion tons of MSW a year[1].

1. The World Bank, 2012. WHAT A WASTE: A Global Review of Solid Waste Management

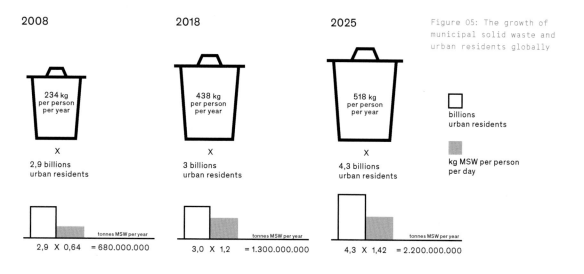

Figure 05: The growth of municipal solid waste and urban residents globally

This calls for a profound change of modus operandi in the current thinking about sustainability, moving away from the classic perception of resource scarcity and limited competition, towards a world where we have all the resources we need. All it takes is a change of viewpoint. Because waste as a concept is nothing but a historical parenthesis; it did not exist before our great technological leap forward, and it is not going to exist in the future either. In other words, waste is a temporary. A once valuable resource caught in a limbo of being useless; but only because we haven't unlocked its potential to become useful again. Perhaps even at a higher value than before. For too long, we have allowed resources to end up as waste – out of sight, out of mind. But we can no longer turn the blind eye to the anomaly of waste generation. So, let's begin the change.

Design the world of tomorrow with the waste of today.

While working towards designing a world without waste.

Currently, there is a strong consensus about what waste is – built into the core structures of society and taught to us from a young age. You know it from your everyday life, when, most days, you will probably end up dumping your left-over meals into the trash can. From the moment we actively chose to throw something out, we change our perception of food from being a valuable resource to becoming waste material.

Our bodies too react. Imagine how you would physically respond if you had to take the left-over food products out of the trash can and have another go at them as edible resources. Well, to some people this may not sound so bad, and the concept of dumpster-diving in huge supermarket containers has actually become a popular trend. Nevertheless, we are not suggesting that everyone should start doing the same. All we are trying to say is that, in order to create more regenerative cities and societies, we ought to change the current stark distinction between what is a resource and what is a waste. Shifting to a circular economy requires that we change our general perception and modify our behaviour. Otherwise, we won't be able to explore the huge potential in old buildings and excess industrial materials that could lead to great reductions of our CO2-emissions.

DESIGNING WITH TWO
OPPOSED IDEAS IN MIND?

In the transition from a linear to a circular economy we must carry out two tasks at once. First, we have to start reactivating the enormous amount of waste humankind has accumulated over the past many decades, centuries and millennia. And while doing so, we must also start designing for circularity, that is, making sure our resources never become waste in the first place.

Looking to design for solutions is nothing new. It has always been our (as well as other organisms') go-to for a survival strategy. Just visit (or revisit) *Biomimicry: Innovation Inspired by Nature*[2], the great book by Janine Benyus, in which she describes how humans have copied nature's models with great success when solving problems in our Industrialised world.

2. Innovation Inspired by Nature. Janine Benyus 2002, William Morrow Paperbacks

In essence, design enables us to create the future we want by making new innovations. It opens up our world and gives us the ability to question our choices, constraints and previous beliefs and perspectives. Design allows us to view the world through different glasses, seeing opportunity where once we would only have seen obstacles.

The involvement of design in how we fundamentally shape our world does not happen automatically. With the rise of the industrialisation, the development phases of an object (whether it is a teacup, a spaceship or a school building) are often left to financial analysts, real-estate developers and engineers, while design usually come either way too late in the process, usually as add-ons to make the desired object look better, or as part of the initial phase only to be discarded later on in the process. From a circular perspective, however, design and architecture are themselves solutions to grand global environmental challenges, and they should be part of the value chain at an earlier stage than now. But that also implies a big responsibility for architects and designers in general, as they must take action to make themselves relevant. It is crucial that they start taking responsibility not only for implementing their designs, but for actually succeeding in making those designs beautiful, aesthetic, functional, affordable and environmentally relevant for the future.

That is why we want to make the case for a collaborative effort among design professionals, and business, financial and educational institutions to empower the designers to take circularity into account. In a sense, that means going "old school" and seeing the value in the *intentionality*, as well as the sense of artistry, that lies in the design. When we do that, even a small building or design object can contain the solution that the world is looking for. Therefore, it should only be natural to start questioning our own choices, especially when it comes to geopolitical and global challenges, giving them greater impact and value. For example, by seeing waste as a future resource for building apartment houses and cities. By seeing potentials where others see none – and by doing something about it.

"The Climate Generation", that's what we call the next wave of children who will grow up learning about a threat vastly different from the one faced by previous generations. It will not be war, terror or economic crisis that will scare them the most. It will be climate change. Climate change caused by the unintentional wrongdoing of their parents, grandparents and great-grandparents, who created a world of hyper-consumption based on a linear model of production and growth.

For the climate generation, education could be the natural starting point for change. By teaching our future economists, politicians, designers, consultants, engineers and architects about the potential locked in what we today see as waste, we can ensure that they see their potentials in light of the opportunities of circular economy.

Some have suggested that the change of mindset entails a downright declaration of 'war on climate change', while others are calling for revolution in the name of stopping global warming[3]. We tend to take a slightly different approach, trying to find the positive aspects of this, at times, hopeless situation.

3. Godoy, E. & Jaffe, A., 2016. We Don't Need a 'War' on Climate Change, We Need a Revolution, The New York Times

DESIGNING YOUR VALUE CHAIN

As we have said, we do not only want designers to be part of the value chain at an earlier stage than now. We want all professions to be able to navigate within different parts of the value chain – brought in appropriately when possible, not just based on out-dated traditions and old habits. In a world where the only constant is change, managing your value chain based on tradition is not going to give you the agility to survive the 4th industrial revolution.

One example from our daily life comes from Anders' training as an architect. For architects, demolition workers are normally not given much thought as they are only a part of the final stage of the value chain – brought in when a building is no longer needed and has to be torn down. But going back to our two principles of *Design the world of tomorrow with the waste of today* while at the same time *designing a world without waste*, demolition workers become a key collaborator for the architect/designer. In fact, they are the first people Anders calls, since they have the materials that we will eventually build with. Thus, they play a huge role in guiding our design towards a world without waste.

Just imagine what we can do if we intentionally put our best efforts toward mitigating climate change. If you are in doubt about the possibilities, just look at how much impact (albeit negative) we were able to do without even realising it.

When it comes to designing for disassembly as well as for flexible modular building, demolition workers are crucial. That's why we see them as the oil sheiks of our time. As they have the access to the resources of the future. Eventually, everyone will see that we have all the resources we need to build our world of tomorrow. Yet just like the oil sheiks, the current demolition workers and waste managers risk becoming obsolete unless they find a way to change our business models and role in society. We will return to this issue later.

EVERY OBSTACLE IS AN OPPORTUNITY

Design is a powerful tool for change. Not just change for the sake of change, but to ensure that we create a prosperous world for all of us. There are two reasons for using design to change the way we use and value our resources. First, climate change is happening at a rapid pace, and, as a global society, we need to act quickly if we want to avoid fatal changes to our environment and livelihood. But, second, mitigating disaster is not the only urgent issue for changemakers and businesses. It is as much a matter of reaping the advantages of being a first mover and taking part in creating the future of business. This means adapting to the changing world order, which has come not only from climate change but also from technological development, the 4th industrial revolution and increased urbanisation.

Thus, we must seize the opportunity that requires a combination of design and innovation. To emphasise this point, we will use the next section of the book to look into how we go from idea to design innovations. With one clear purpose: Creating the future we want – a future for all to prosper in without compromise.

We see design as a philosophy, as a method of creating change, just as we see innovation as the way to reap the benefits and make that change happen from a practical perspective. Or as MIT professors Eugene Fitzgerald, Andreas Wanker and Carl Schramm put it: "Innovation is the embodiment of a useful idea in the marketplace"[4] – a result achievable through an iterative process moving between technology, marketing and implementation.

4. Fitzgerald, Wanker & Schram, 2011. Inside Real Innovation

Technology is generally understood as the product or process of development. Through our circular-economy glasses, the innovation might as well be the change from a product business model to a service business model, or from changing the supply used in production from virgin material to circulated material. Which leads us to our next point: change is not always about creating something fundamentally new. It might as well just be to see things with new eyes.

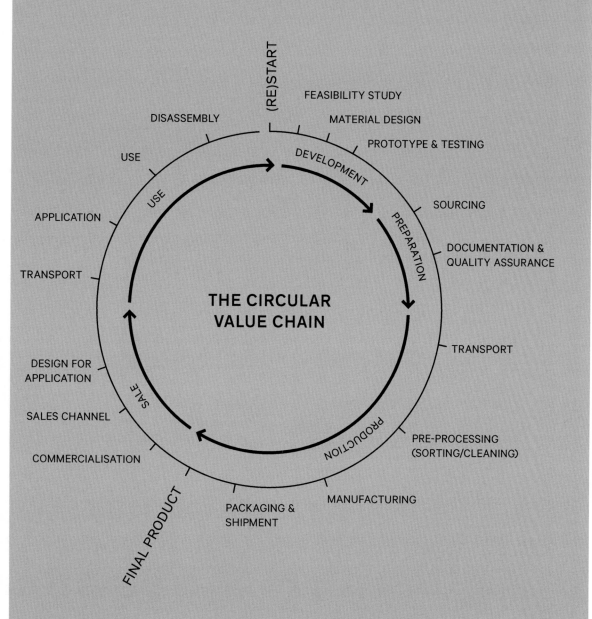

Upcycled concrete, windows and wood - Upcycle Studios truly captures the very
essence of upcycling.

UPCYCLE STUDIOS

Welcome to the world's first commercially scaled circular residental project.

As our cities are expanding and the majority of the world population are now living an urban life – we find ourselves standing on a crossroad. On the one hand, we are going to need more housing and office spaces than ever before. On the other, we must accept that we cannot just build more and more in the way we have been used to without also increasing the negative footprint on our climate significantly. And that calls for a change.

Luckily, several trends and conditions are making way for a solution to solve these global challenges at once – without compromising on either the rising demands for buildings in the city or the urgent need to mitigate climate change.

First of all, our global approach to work have changed in recent years. Entrepreneurs are the new rockstars, millennials don't feel the need for a steady job, and WeWork, providing shared officespaces and flexible working communities is about to be the second highest valued start-up company in the United States. Much like in the rest of the world the entrepreneurial spirit has increased in the metropolitan area of Copenhagen. At the same time, for the modern and urban family, the pursuit of the perfect work-life-balance has taken new form. The dream of the "good life" is now deeply connected to flexibility, freedom and purpose – and the classical "nine-to-five" life is phased out in favor of a symbiosis between "working" and "living". For the same family awareness of a need to protect our climate and a desire to live sustainable is increasing as well and concepts such as the sharing economy and resource optimisation are gaining popularity.

And this is where it really gets interesting. Because currently, we underutilise our buildings in the cities big time. One estimate for example suggests that only 35-40 % of all office spaces in Europe are fully utilised during working hours[5]. And offices are not the only types of underutilised buildings in the city. Half of all private homes are 'under-occupied' – having at least two bedrooms more than what is really needed[6]. In Denmark alone, Ellen McArthur foundation estimates that better sharing of buildings, the combining of their purposes and increasing their availability holds a potential net-value of $125-172 million every year from 2035[7].

5. Ellen MacArthur Foundation, 2015. Growth within: a circular economy vision for a competitive Europe

6. Ellen MacArthur Foundation, 2015. Delivering the circular economy: A toolkit for policymakers

7. Ibid.

Therefore, we came up with the idea of Upcycle Studios – building the house of tomorrow with the waste of today. Located in the upcoming Ørestad South district of Copenhagen, Upcycle Studios is a block of 20 townhouses based on the circular economy; reflected in the project's high degree of flexibility and in the materials used to build it. To start out with, each home in Upcycle Studios – divided onto 3 floors – can be used as combined housing and workspace. For creative freelancers, for self-employed entrepreneurs, and for a large family with various daily rhythms, routines and interests. The freedom to divide the apartment into separate spaces and areas allows the owner to rent out different parts of the house permanently or for a shorter period of time. This ensures the best possible use of the homes at all hours of the day and in different phases of life.

Now, while coming up with a concept for a building that is way easier to utilise to its full extend – we did so by taking care of three other major issues at the same time: resource scarcity, inconceivable waste accumulation and climate change. To lay the foundation of Upcycle Studios, we took in 1400 tons of waste concrete from the expansion of the Copenhagen Metro and upcycled it.

This was enough to substitute almost half of the new concrete – eliminating a waste challenge and reducing the emission of CO_2 at the same time. By using this aggregate from old, crushed concrete, we save 12-15% CO_2 per ton. This might not be the most impressive reduction, but when thinking of the massive scale of concrete we use today, it could add up to a global saving on 2 billion tons of CO_2 annually – 12 times the Danish yearly CO_2-emissions.

And there is good reason to be better at reactivating old, used concrete. Apart from water, concrete is the most commonly used material in the world[8]. This has been true for a long time, and global trends suggest it will remain so in the future. It is estimated that 60% of the buildings needed to handle the current levels of population growth and urbanisation have not even been built yet[9]. And technically, using more concrete and building more houses in a rapid pace to keep up with the demand is possible. Just look at China where it only took three years (2011-2013) to use more concrete than the US did throughout the entire 20th century[10]. But, we have to keep in mind that cement (a main ingredient of concrete) is already responsible for almost 6% of the global CO_2-emissions right now[11]. And this could easily become worse if we continue doing business – and buildings – as usual. That is exactly why we are trying to lead the way with Upcycle Studios – getting more by using less.

Another example of how we applied circular economy to the project of Upcycle Studios is the usage of old window glass – taken from abandoned buildings in the Northern part of Denmark. In fact, 75% of all windows in the new dwellings – as the name indicates – are upcycled as well. If you wonder what impact that makes, the upcycled glass saves 96% CO_2 compared to using new glass. The emissions are even further reduced by making all window frames out of certified, sustainable

8. World Business Council for Sustainable Development, 2009. The Cement Sustainability Initiative

9. Clos, J., 2016. The opportunity to build tomorrow's cities. World Economic Forum

10. Swanson, A., 2015. How China used more cement in 3 years than the U.S. did in the entire 20th Century. The Washington Post

11. Harvey, F., 2018. Cement industry urged to reduce 'invisible' global emissions. The Guardian

75% of all windows in Upcycle Studios are made from old double-glazed windows. By layering two double-glazed windows, we createa new window that fully complies with the official requirements for energy efficiency.

wood instead of aluminum, which would typically have been preferred in this type of project.

On top of that, all floors, wall coverings and façades on Upcycle Studios are produced by off-cut wood waste from the exclusive Danish wood manufacturer named Dinesen. Besides from the ability to reuse an obviously valuable resource, doing so also eliminates all use of chemicals in otherwise needed paints, sealants, silicone, lime and wallpaper. Keeping all materials natural and healthy for a sustainable indoor climate.

UPCYCLE STUDIOS
Type: Residential
Area: 3000 square metres
Site: Ørestad, Denmark
Client: NREP A/S
and Arkitektgruppen A/S
Main contractor: Arkitektgruppen A/S
Engineer: MOE A/S
Architect: Lendager ARC
Status: Finished in 2018
Year: 2015 -
Partner in charge: Anders Lendager
Project leader: Jesper Høiberg
Team: Mathias Ruø Rasmussen,
Anette Orth Laybourn, Nicholas Ransome,
Iben Nørkjær, Torben Vestergaard,
Niklas Nolsøe, Sunniva Garshol,
Signe Balthazar Munk

1400 tons of waste concrete from the expansion of the subway line in Copenhagen gets new life and value in Upcycle Studios.

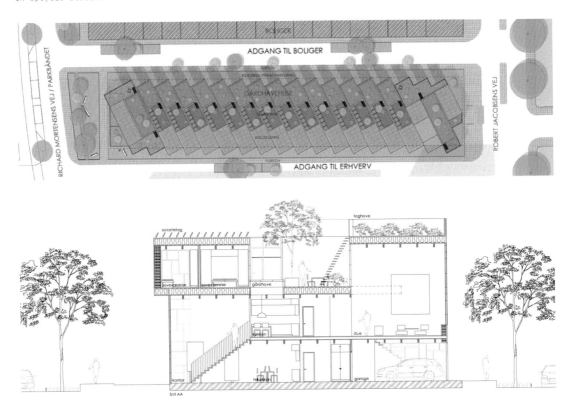

All the upcycled materials for the project was processed by our own "UP" production company in Lendager group which is specialised in upcycle product development and innovation, constantly innovating our waste fractions into the most important building materials.

By building on the circular design principles that *waste is more* and *local is global*, it was possible to lower emissions and avoid using as many virgin materials as possible - all without compromising on neither aesthetics, price nor quality. With Upcycle Studios, our goal was always to reach for the stars making sure that the project was not only doing less bad than traditional construction but in fact part of the solution – contributing positively to our global well-being.

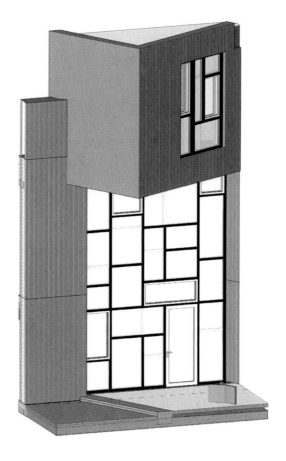

Old glass is fitted with new frames to create an upcycled floor-to-ceiling window. This saves 96% CO2 compared to new glass.

ADDED VALUE

To be honest, we count our blessings for being Danes and having the perspective gained from growing up in the Danish welfare state. However, from a professional point of view, there are two traditions we are particularly fond of, continuously exposed to and participating in. First comes the strong Danish tradition of encouraging sustainable businesses and to see the potential for such ventures. The Danish wind adventure is a perfect example of this where business and the renewal energy transition are prerequisites. Second is the exceptional quality of our design. With our unique Danish mind-set about the use of green technology for sustainable business and our world-class aesthetics, we have a unique opportunity to use circular economy to create socially responsible solutions for business and the environment.

We have allowed ourselves to be inspired by other creative forces within Denmark, such as the film industry and the new Nordic cuisine, and come up with a manifesto for circular design. We originally created it as an internal guideline – particularly for buildings and architecture – but we hope it will have value in a broader sense.

THE MANIFESTO
DESIGNING FOR CIRCULARITY

REACH FOR THE STARS

The innovation must not compromise on quality, aesthetics or price.

LOCAL IS GLOBAL

The innovation must utilise local resources.

BE THE SOLUTION

The innovation must have a positive impact on society.

PEOPLE MATTER

The innovation must be socially sustainable by respecting
and engaging individuals from all ethnic groups and social classes.

CITY IS NATURE

The innovation must respect and enhance the
biodiversity of the environment.

BODY LANGUAGE

The innovation must see itself as part of a larger metabolic
system, taking all resources into account and contributing
to and interacting with them.

—

Like the film industry and the gourmet-cuisine movement, we use our
manifesto as creative constraints in our innovation process affirming
that design and creativity have functional as well as aesthetic value and
that our goal is to provide solutions without compromise. In the next
chapter, we will give you examples of how we do it.

1.1.1   House demolition.

PROCESS / MATERIALS   1. BRICK

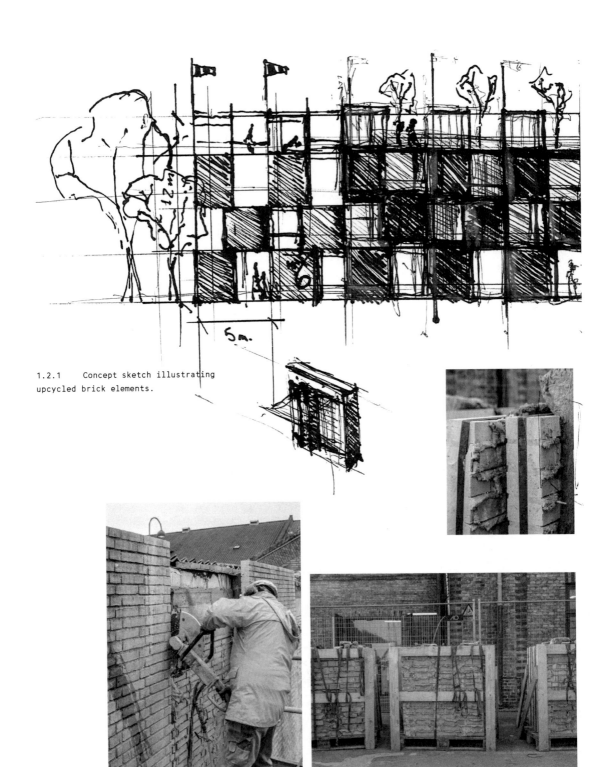

1.2.1   Concept sketch illustrating
upcycled brick elements.

1.2.2   Brick elements cut from
buildings that would otherwise be ready
for demolition.

1.2.3   Cut-out brick elements in mold.

THE BUILDING

The buidling was very suitable for creating upcycled wall elements due to the particularly hard cement mortar between the bricks.

CUTTING PROCESS

The building turned out to be double walled. One side had to be dismounted by hand before the other side could be cut out. This manual process proved to be very time consuming.

MODULE

The module was laid horizontally after cutting, which caused breakage and cracks. This method was therefore abandoned.

FOUR MODULES IN PLACE

One day and two craftsmen was what it took to cut out four modules. The modules were then ready to be tested for different stabilization, suspension methods, etc.

MODULE WITH REINFORCEMENT

The modules were shaped by molding back sides as stabilizing elements to prevent further cracks and collapse when installed.

MODULE WITH CAST BACK

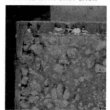

As a start, one of the module's back was molded with recycled concrete. The test showed whether the concrete acted as a stabilizing element and gave an idea of the total mass.

1.2.4   Finished upcycled wall element.

1.3.1   Muuratsalo Experimental House opened by Alvar Aalto in 1952 - example of and inspiration for experimental use of bricks.

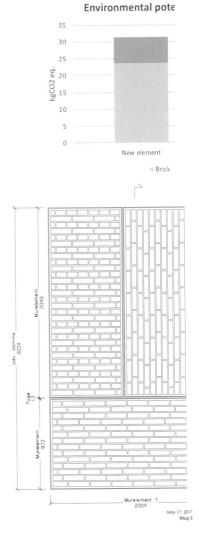

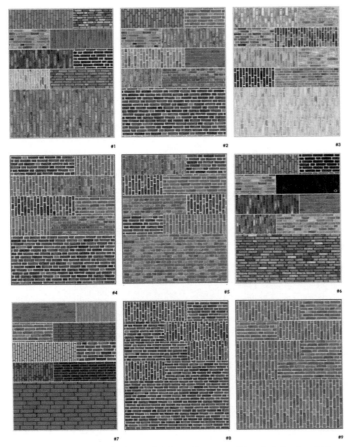

#1 #2 #3

#4 #5 #6

#7 #8 #9

1.3.2   Different design solutions for upcycling brick elements.

1.3.3   Wall element casted into concrete.

1.3.4   Examples of brick experiments at the Wasteland Exhibition.

1.3.5   Bricks in production.

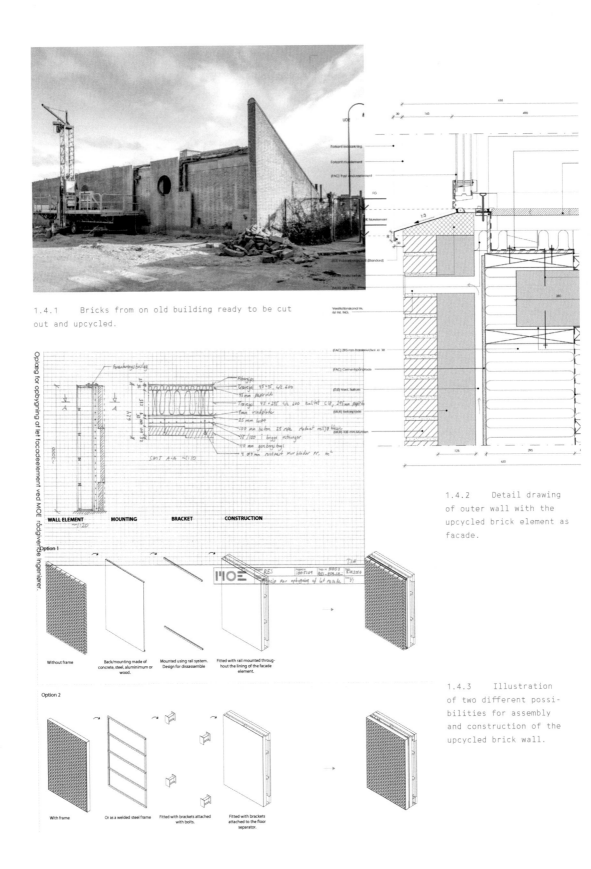

1.4.1   Bricks from on old building ready to be cut out and upcycled.

1.4.2   Detail drawing of outer wall with the upcycled brick element as facade.

1.4.3   Illustration of two different possibilities for assembly and construction of the upcycled brick wall.

WALL ELEMENT   MOUNTING   BRACKET   CONSTRUCTION

Option 1

Without frame

Back/mounting made of concrete, steel, aluminium or wood.

Mounted using rail system. Design for disassemble

Fitted with rail mounted throughout the lining of the facade element.

Option 2

With frame

Or as a welded steel frame

Fitted with brackets attached with bolts.

Fitted with brackets attached to the floor separator.

1.4.4   The upcycled brick wall elements under construction on the Resource Rows.

2.2.1
Upcycled concrete: From
old building to gravel to
new building.

Existing building
environmentally screened
and recovered

Building crushed roughly

Transportation for de

P1: 0-4 mm

P1: 4-25 mm

P1: >25 mm

P2: 0-4 mm

P2: 4-25 mm

P2: >25 mm

2.2.2   Crushed concrete sorted in different fractions.

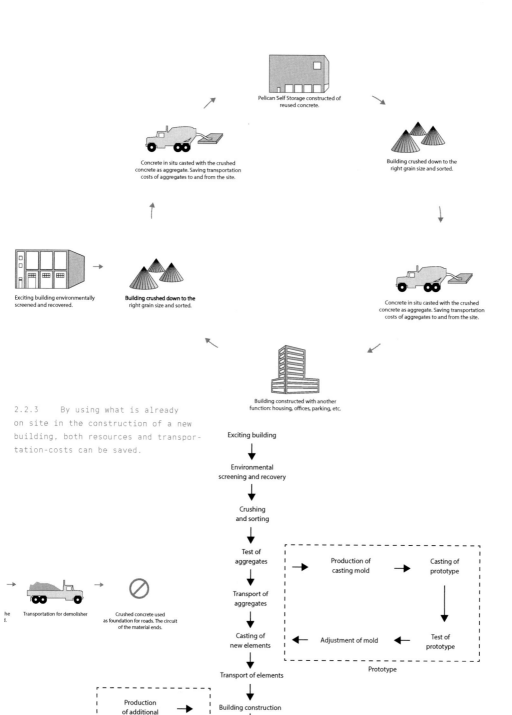

Pelican Self Storage constructed of reused concrete.

Concrete in situ casted with the crushed concrete as aggregate. Saving transportation costs of aggregates to and from the site.

Building crushed down to the right grain size and sorted.

Exciting building environmentally screened and recovered.

Building crushed down to the right grain size and sorted.

Concrete in situ casted with the crushed concrete as aggregate. Saving transportation costs of aggregates to and from the site.

Building constructed with another function: housing, offices, parking, etc.

2.2.3   By using what is already on site in the construction of a new building, both resources and transportation-costs can be saved.

Transportation for demolisher

Crushed concrete used as foundation for roads. The circuit of the material ends.

Exciting building

↓

Environmental screening and recovery

↓

Crushing and sorting

↓

Test of aggregates

↓

Transport of aggregates

↓

Casting of new elements

↓

Transport of elements

↓

Building construction

↓

Registration of the building

↓

Use of the building

↓

End of life / Transformation

Production of casting mold → Casting of prototype

↓

Adjustment of mold ← Test of prototype

Prototype

Production of additional elements →

↑

CE marking upcycle element

↑

KS concrete element ←

2.3.1   Upcycled concrete loaded on to a concrete pump directly on site.

2.3.2   The concrete is produced at the construction site on a mobile
concrete mixing plant.

2.3.3   Cast-in-situ concrete process
using recycled concrete.

Material	Weight [g]	Content [weight %]
Concrete	2,467.3	79
Stone aggregates	569.6	18
Brick	97.3	3
Glass	0.2	0
Total	3,134.4	100

Material	Volume [cm³]	Proportions [cm³/kg]
Wood pieces, liquid	1.2	1.7

Result of hand petrographic analysis according to DS/EN 933-11 for 4-22 mm-fraction

Sieve size [mm]		Requirements for fall-through		Fall-through		Are require-ments met?
		[weight, %]	[tolerance, %]	[weight, %]	[tolerance, %]	
20	44	100		100		OK
1.40	31	93-100		100		OK
D	22	90-99		100		OK
D/2	11	25-70	±17.5	53	±10	OK
d	4	0-15		10		OK
d/2	2	0-5		7		No

Requirements for rough aggregates of the type Gc90/15, cf. DS/EN 12620 table 2 and 3 compared with measured values

Test ID	Apparent density [kg/m³]	Density, dry [kg/m³]	Density, w.s.d. [kg/m³]	Absorption [%]
1	2,585	2,335	2,432	4.1
2	2,584	2,347	2,439	3.9
Mean value	2,584	2,341	2,435	4.0

Density and water absorption for 4-22 mm material

Partial test nr.	Na₂O [mass %]
1-1	0.004
1-2	0.003
Mean value	0.003

Content of water soluble alkalis for 4-22 mm material

Partial test nr.	Chloride content [mass %]
1-1	0.004
1-2	0.004
Mean value	0.004

Chloride content for 4-22 mm material

2.4.2   Technical results of the sieve analysis and declaration of the recycled concrete aggregate (Pelcon).

2.4.3   Assembly of concrete wall elements in Upcycle Studios.

2.4.4   Construction in process.

2.4.5   Upcycled con-
crete with crushed bricks
as aggregate.

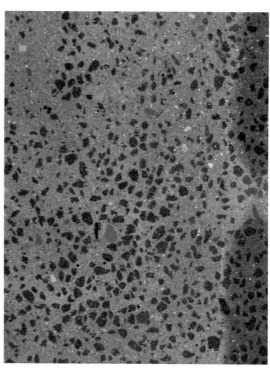

2.5.1   Internal wall element at Upcycle Studios.

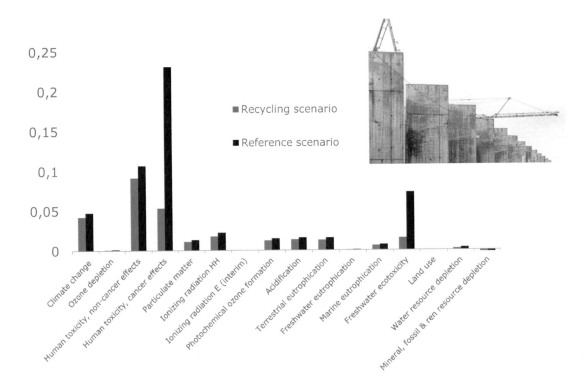

2.5.2   Close-up of concrete sample.

2.5.3   The concrete mix expert
performs quality assurance and control
on site.

2.5.4   Upcycle Studios construction site.

2.6.1   The upcycled wall elements
in Upcycle Studios are visible from
the inside.

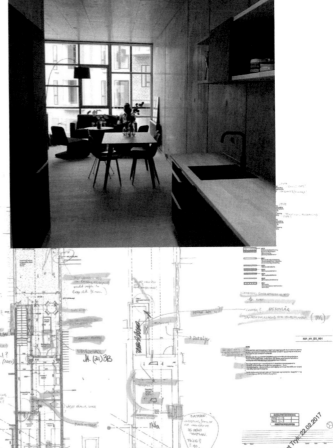

k01_H5_EX_N07

2.6.2   In addition to upcycled concrete, Upcycle Studios is also made of upcycled windows and wood panels.

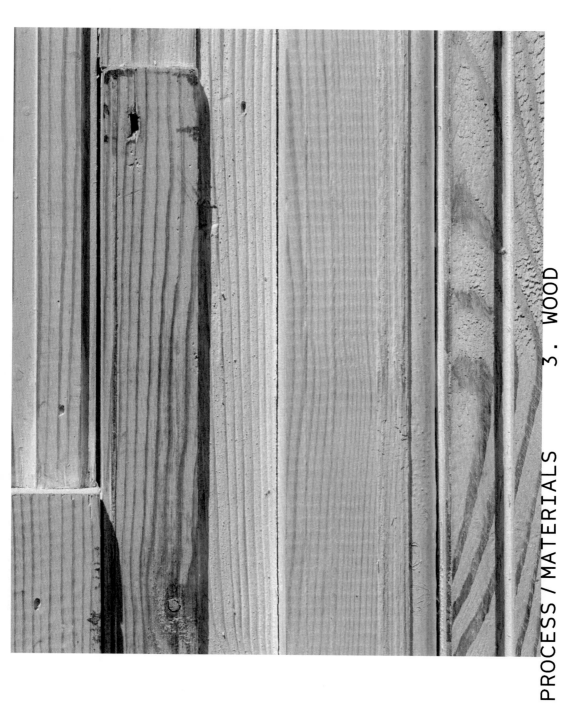

PROCESS / MATERIALS   3. WOOD

3.2.2   Waste wood form the expansion of the Copenhagen Metro. Normally, the wood would be incinerated, but in this case the wood is upcycled.

3.2.1   Old rafters used again for Stedsans In The Woods - an outdoor resort and restaurant in Sweden.

3.2.3   By charring the surface with fire we impregnate the wood to make it resistant to fire, insects and fungus without using any chemicals.

3.2.4   The technique comes from Japan and is called Yakisugi.

3.2.5   The reused wood is used as
facade cladding at the Resource Rows.

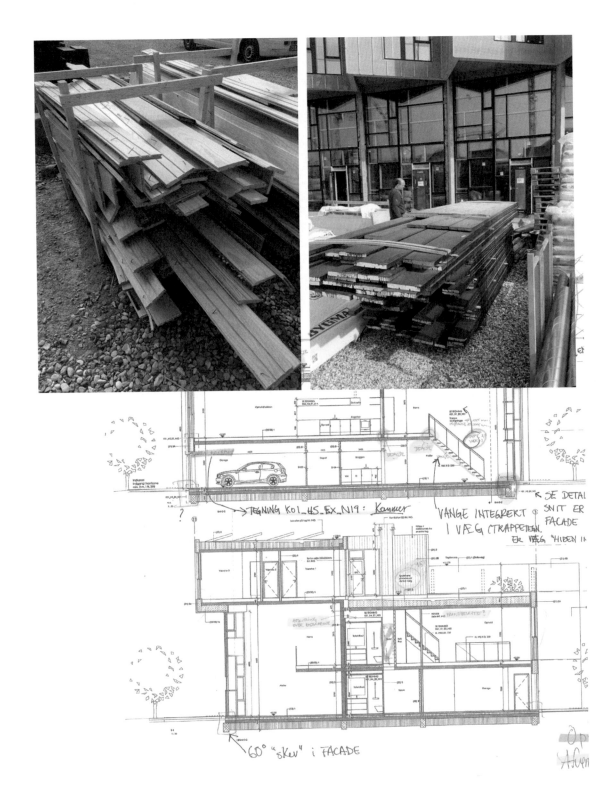

→ TEGNING K01_H5_EX_N19: Kammer

VANGE INTEGRERT ○ SNIT ER

I VÆG (TRAPPETRIN

ER VÆG "HIDEN IN

SE DETAL

FACADE

60° "skev" i FACADE

3.3.1   Blue stained wood planks are
treated with black linseed oil to make
use of planks that otherwise would have
been discarded.

3.3.2   The upcycled wooden planks are used as facade on Upcycle Studios.

3.4.2   Off-cuts from
the Danish high-end
floor manufacturer Dinesen
– used for floors and
wall covering in Upcycle
Studios.

3.4.1   Inside the
first rowhouse of Upcycle
Studios.

3. WOOD

3.4.3   Charred upcycle wood
used as wall covering inside
a Danish summer cabin.

PROCESS / MATERIALS

3.5.1   Old windows
are harvested from empty
buildings or renovations
around Denmark.

The wooden frames are
then upcyled and used as
indoor wall coverings.

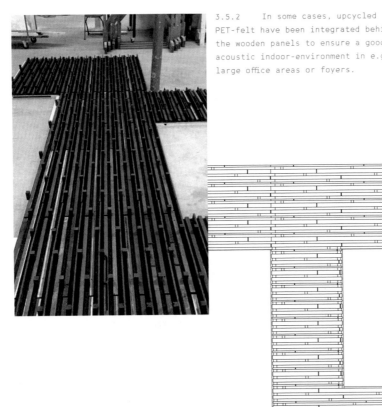

3.5.2   In some cases, upcycled
PET-felt have been integrated behind
the wooden panels to ensure a good
acoustic indoor-environment in e.g.
large office areas or foyers.

3.5.3   Test of panels for Epic Skanska.

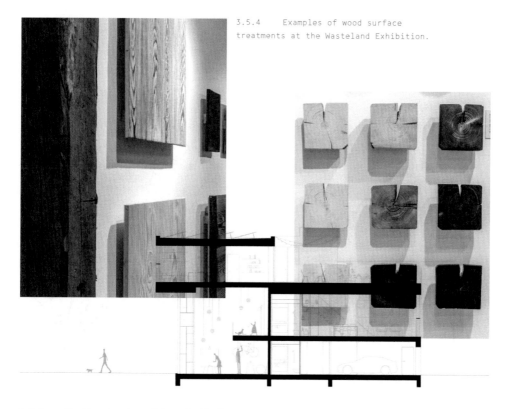

3.5.4   Examples of wood surface
treatments at the Wasteland Exhibition.

3.5.5   Section drawing of Upcycle Studios.

3.5.6   Upcycled wall panels made of old window frames installed in Copenhagen Towers II.

PROCESS / MATERIALS   4. GLASS

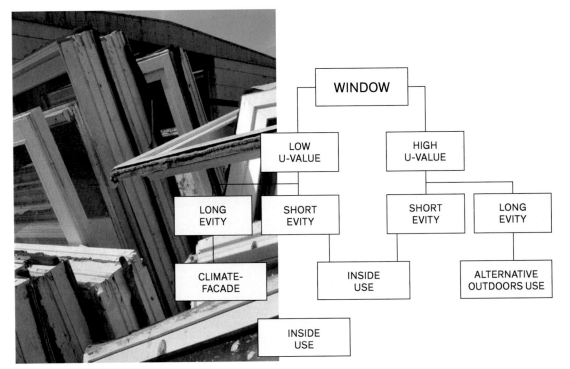

4.2.1   Recommended ways to recycle windows in order to obtain the largest economic and material value as possible.

Bestemmelse af g₄

Rudens solenergitransmittans (g_t-værdien) siger hvor stor del af solens samlede spektrum, som passerer en rude. Nedenfor er vist illustration af dette for en almindelig to-lags energirude.

Figur 21: Illustration af solenergitransmittans

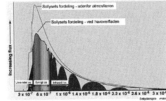

Figur 22: Sollysets fordeling. Til gg bestemmelse anvendes det samlede solspektrum.

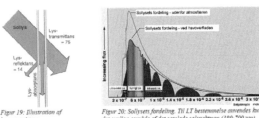

Figur 19: Illustration af lystransmittans

Figur 20: Sollysets fordeling. Til LT bestemmelse anvendes kun det synlige område af det samlede solspektrum (380-700 nm).

4.2.3   Illustration of solar transmittance and distribution of sunlight through energy glazing.

4.2.2   Upcycle windows tested and approved by Technological Institute.

4.2.4   Upcycled window-glass detached from the old frames. The frames will be used in other upcycle projects.

Genbrug af vinduer (2015-krav)
Miljømæssigt potentiale

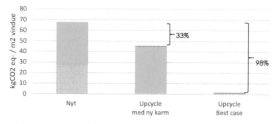

33%

98%

▫ Rude   ▪ Karmkonstruktion   ▪ Transport af brugte vinduer   ▪ Klargøring/oprensning

Genbrug af vinduer (2020-krav)
Miljømæssigt potentiale

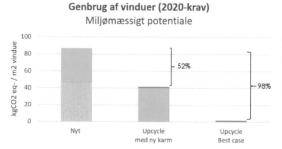

52%

98%

▫ Rude   ▪ Karmkonstruktion   ▪ Transport af brugte vinduer   ▪ Klargøring/oprensning

4.2.5   Preliminary calculations of the potential CO_2-savings when upcycling old windows.

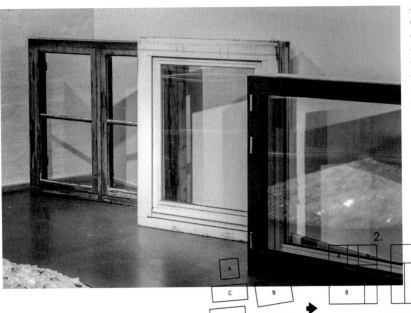

4.3.1   Four types of upcycled window-glass are collected in elements. In case of empty fields, new glass will complement the elements. At last, the elements are assembled in whole window sections.

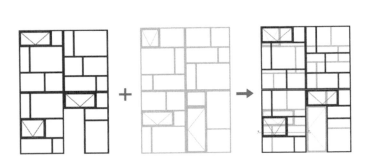

4.3.2   Two double-glazed window elements are layered together as one floor-to-ceiling window - functioning as a building envelope.

4.3.3   Mock-up of an upcycled window element at the Wasteland Exhibition.

4.3.4   Inside Upcycle Studios. Double-layered window installed from upcycled glass
- performing in accordance with the Danish 2020 building regulations.

4.4.1   Work in progress. Mounting the upcycle windows at Upcycle Studios.

4.4.2   Upcycled window elements installed in Upcycle Studios.

4.4.3   Render of the window patchwork
in Upcycle Studios.

5. PLASTIC

PROCESS / MATERIALS

5.2.1   PET felt made of old PET plastic bottles
- used for acoustic panels in Copenhagen Towers II.

5.2.2   Only 9 percent of all plastic
waste is recycled today - meaning
that we currently have 5 billion tons
of plastic waste either piled up on
landfills or spread out in nature and
into our oceans.

5.2.3   The acoustic panels installed inside Copenhagen Towers II.

6.2.1   The facade is made from upcycled beer and soda cans of aluminum.

6.2.2   The foundation for Upcycle House is built with recycled screw piles in steel.

Put together from a long range of different upcycle materials such as nylon, paper, wood, cork, plastic, windows and Cellulose insulation, the Upcycle House saves 86% carbon-emissions in the construction phase compared to a benchmark house built from new materials.

6.2.3   Upcycle House was built on a subplot that is developed by Realdania By og Byg to showcase different approaches to sustainable building practice.

6.3.1   In the renovation of Falkonercentret, the steel plates are taken down and re-designed to give a more modern look on the building.

6.3.2   Normally, the old plates would have been thrown out and melted for new purposes.

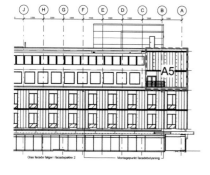

6.3.3   When the old steel plates are renovated they all go back on the facade of the old congress hall and hotel.

6.3.4   1.400 stainless steel-plates - equal to 2.000 square metres - are renovated and re-mounted on the Falkoner Center in Frederiksberg, Denmark.

6.4.1   The renovation of Falkonercentret in progress.

6.4.2   In redesigning the old plates, the steel
is glass blasted, primed and powder coated. The edges
are cut off and the plates are then folded. Lastly,
the surface and plate quality are checked.

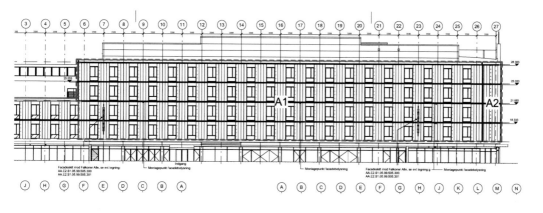

6.4.3   Calculating the impact from renovating the
old steel, each recycled plate makes up a saving of
35 kilo CO2. That's almost 60 tonnes of CO2 in total.

1.2.1   Stedsans in the Woods.
Far away from city lights and traffic
noise, in the woods of Sweden, you
find a permaculture farm with a restaurant
and small cabins - made by natural
and upcycled materials.

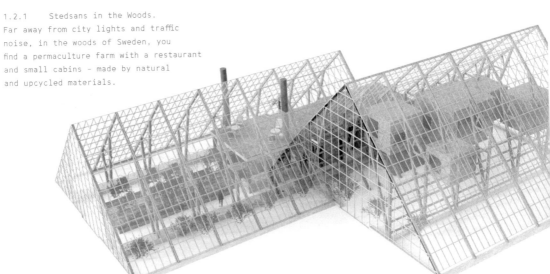

1.2.2   In Lisbjerg on the outskirts of Aarhus, Denmark, Lendager Group develops a project that delves deeply into resource efficiency and explores how resource thinking can add value and character to greenfield building projects.

The project is called 'Made in Aarhus' and is an example of how urban metabolism and ambitious resource thinking can create new housing areas that addresses two issues at one time: climate change as well as the individual's right to light, clean air, human scale and a strong sense of belonging.

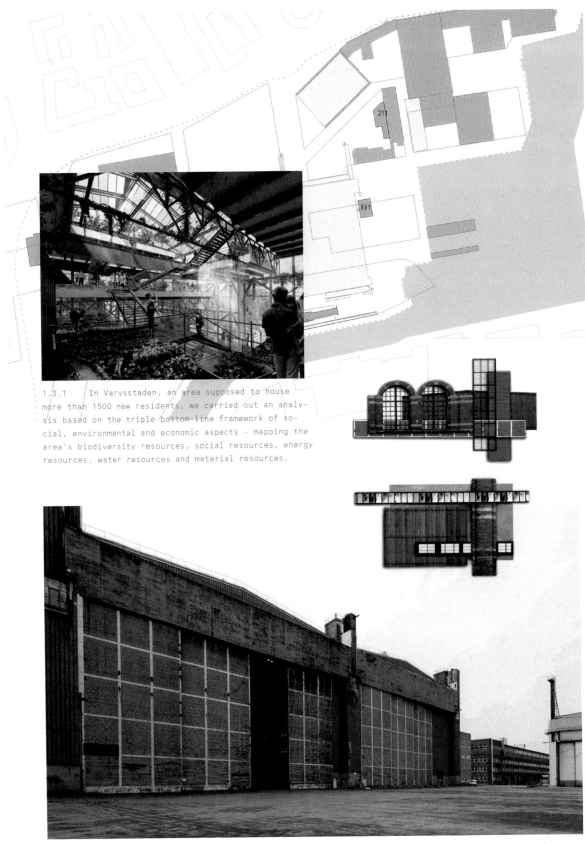

1.3.1 In Varvsstaden, an area supposed to house more than 1500 new residents, we carried out an analysis based on the triple bottom-line framework of social, environmental and economic aspects – mapping the area's biodiversity resources, social resources, energy resources, water resources and material resources.

1.3.2 During its heyday in the 1950s and 1960s, Malmö's western harbour was home to the world's biggest shipyard - employing more than 6000 workers.

1.3.3   In the South Harbour of Aarhus, we are going to transform the old Coal Crane Bridge to a new, green pathway connecting the harbour area with the rest of the city.

1.3.4   Fanø Beach House embraces all the activities of the beach and the surrounding nature.

1.3.5   A common dining house in Grøntorvet, where excess materials constantly move from one system to another, thus completely eliminating the idea of waste.

"There is nothing more difficult to take in hand, more perilous to conduct, or more uncertain in its success, than to take the lead in the introduction of the new order of things. Because the innovator has for enemies all those who have done well under the old conditions, and lukewarm defenders in those who might do well under the new"

Niccolò Machiavelli, The Prince

EXPERIENCES FROM
THE FRONTIERS OF
THE BUILT ENVIRONMENT

Doing things differently is tough. Nonetheless it is exactly what we need to do. We have to change the rules of the game and start creating businesses and buildings that give more than they take. That means being "best in class" is no longer enough. Instead we must innovate and create a new way of being, a new school of doing. So how do we take the step from doing less bad to doing good?

First of all, let's be clear: No one understands the entire picture of how to truly create a regenerative, prosperous future where climate change is mitigated and the global population is thriving. Yet many people know bits and pieces. Lots of innovation still need to happen, and lots of dots still need to be connected, which is why creating partnerships and combining forces across the value chain and with researchers, philanthropic institutions and governments are crucial.

Our goal is to move not only towards sustainable construction but toward societal sustainability through the built environment with scalable global solutions benefitting citizens, societies and businesses. We intend to give the built environment a key role in solving global challenges – serving as pioneering examples of how construction can be the driving force of the UN's Sustainable Development Goals.

Therefore, the built environment should not only be sustainable in its own right – in terms of using resources in a responsible way during construction – but also facilitate the sustainability of our physical and mental health, our communities and the way we create regenerative urban environments. A lever for other industries showing the way forward, going from obstacle to opportunity.

Easier said than done, one might say. And yes, it certainly is.

Changing the rules of the game or to "introduce a new order of things" as Machiavelli put it in the above quote from his masterpiece, *The Prince*, is, as we know from our own work, indeed difficult. Difficult but not impossible and greatly advantageous if successful. The world is calling for change, and it seems we are finally getting ready for it. There is an increasing demand for sustainable solutions, but like all other innovations – not at any cost.

Instead, what we see is that if we are able to change demand and consumption at a pace that mitigates climate change, we must be certain that our sustainable solutions do not compromise on price, aesthetics or convenience. They must generate materials, products and business models, which correlate with both business and climate.

On September 25th, 2015, countries created a set of goals to end poverty, protect the planet, and ensure prosperity for all as part of a new sustainable development agenda. UN, 2015.

In the third and fourth part of this book we introduce you to the strategic tools that will help you create change. But before that, we want to share a few experiences from our own journey in the built environment in the hope that you can learn from them, quickly overcome
the obstacles and conquer the new frontiers of sustainable business and buildings.

FROM VISIONARY IDEA TO TANGIBLE RESULTS:

Building based on the principles of circular economy – using upcy-cled concrete, wood, bricks, windows, plastics, etc. – is the norm in Lendager Group. Yet it is still very new in the industry as a whole. So how did we get there?

It started with the idea that a waste material that could be turned into a resource and the endless repetition of two questions:

Why shouldn't it be possible?
How can we do it?

While Upcycle House was the first house Lendager Group de-signed based on the principles of circular economy, the material innovations really started when we were asked to create "visible sustainability" via the interior materials of the new Copenhagen luxury high-rise: Copenhagen Towers II. Even though this was the most sustainable hotel in Copenhagen, none of the sustainability was visible for their guests and tenants to see or feel. We had to change that.

The developers had come up with an ambitious goal for making the building state-of-the-art with regard to sustainability. So, the fact that the exterior had already been made from traditional concrete struck Anders as odd for two reasons. First, as mentioned earlier on, he knew that traditional concrete had a big environmental foot-print. Second, he was aware that, though 95% of the concrete from demolished buildings is reused and therefore considered (by the concrete industry) to be "sustainable," it is not upcycled for use as a building material but, rather, down-cycled and used as road fill.

But these facts did not deter Anders. Instead they gave him the opportunity to venture out of his architectural comfort zone and become an innovator, producing a new sustainable, upcycled con-crete to construct the floors of Copenhagen Towers II. Much to the surprise and disbelief of the traditional industry (not to mention the pushback they gave him) Anders and the rest of the Lendager team succeeded.

FROM INNOVATION TO IMPLEMENTATION

To give a more precise idea of how we actually made it happen, and not least what obstacles to be mindful of, we asked one of our project managers about his experience with going from innovation to implementation. His know-how comes from another Lendager Group building project in Copenhagen where we used 100% of the concrete from the old building on site to raise the new building with. Doing so, we created a new type of construction site: a circular construction site where the material was sourced and upcycled on-site – smart not only in terms of reuse of the material but also because of the avoided transportation. Here's how he recalls the process:

> **PM:** First of all, it was clear that our partners were not comfortable with our innovative way of doing things. In fact, the subcontractors were very straightforward about this and told us they did not believe it was possible to cast with up-cycled concrete! They said they could only trust the quality of their usual "laser screed" method." They explained they were also concerned that the consistency of the new kind of concrete would vary and thus cause the floor to be bumpy. Because of their lack of confidence in the process, they did not want to be responsible for the project.

> At the same time, we were having a difficult time working the traditional government-approved technological institutes that would normally do the technical tests of materials. The GTS-institutions did not share our optimism when it came to the use of up-cycled concrete. Luckily, we were finally able to get the necessary dispensation from the Copenhagen Municipality as long as we could make sure the standards would be followed. And we could.

> In short, we had more than enough reason to believe that up-cycling the concrete might not be possible after all. We were tempted to give up and say that we had done our best. That we had tried, but faced insurmountable obstacles.

Now, fast-forward to the building site: It is a beautiful, sunny day in December. The new subcontractors are working. Rubber boots on. Cheeks red. And when our project manager introduces himself as being from Lendager Group, big smiles break out on their faces. They are all super-positive about the new material and tell him that the quality is much higher than the traditional concrete. So smooth, and so fresh. That day they succeeded in making more floor than they ever had. The circular building site was a reality!

As we explain in the next chapter, one of our key strengths is always believing something is doable until we have been proved wrong. You might say that when we take on a project, we always have a "presumption of possibility." And so, instead of giving up we kept going, found a way forward, and designed a new type of value chain with the right partners to succeed.

So, the production of the upcycled concrete began.

What have we learned so far:

1. **Strategic alignment across the value chain is necessary.** Don't underestimate the value of being strategically aligned. You must ensure that your stakeholders and the necessary actors are aligned with your vision and share your motives, and, most important, that they are ready and willing to support you when reality hits.

2. **Innovation is not "business as usual".** No matter what your idea is, innovation is never business as usual. Identify the potential barriers, whether they are regulations, lack of partners, old habits or perceived impossibilities. You can use our *business model canvas The Circular Way* as described in part four of the book, to do so. And if you are successful, the added value should far surpass the potential downside of doing something new.

Similarly, without compromising on the final result, be aware that you might need some wiggle-room (that is, flexibility) in the process to figuring out the best way to implement your innovation. Be sure your stakeholders are aware of this.

3. **Material sourcing & the necessary infrastructure.**
Even though you might have identified a large amount of waste (either from outside of or within the building that can be utilised as a resource, it does not necessarily entail that you have the access to it. Gaining continuous access to the given waste resource is key to ensure a steady supply, which in turn, is absolute necessity if we are to be successful at scaling upcycled building materials at the required pace to mitigate climate change.

A tip from us: In Lendager TCW we are currently helping production companies outside the built environment with creating innovations that can turn their waste into wealth in the form of new building materials. That way, they increase their sustainability and get rid of a waste problem. At the same time, they come up with an upcycled material (with a steady flow) that can replace virgin materials and lower the negative externalities in the built environment. This, in turn, will create new jobs that can be done by the skilled workers who are currently in danger of being replaced by technology.

4. **Necessary scale.** Doing something new might make you or your partners want to limit the risks by starting small. While that sounds reasonable, remember that the business case for upcycling is that the bigger the scale of the production, the better. Thus, we encourage you to pay attention to your break-even point, and make sure you and your partners are strategically aligned with respect to when and what it takes to increase production.

A FAIRYTALE OF UPCYCLING

Circular economy, upcycling, disruption, blue-ocean strategy, innovation. Most people think of these slightly hyped and buzzword-sounding terms as contemporary business concepts. But they make us wonder if renowned Danish storyteller Hans Christian Andersen was, in fact, a forerunner of today's organisational oracles and smart consultants when he was writing one of his many stories back in 1855?

We definitely think so! Our approach to innovation and business development is greatly inspired by H. C. Andersen's famous fairy-tale "Klods-Hans" (translated in English as "Jack the Dullard," or "Blockhead Hans."). The protagonist is the typical underdog who exceeds everyone's expectations and overtakes his two brothers, his father's favourites in winning the princess and half the kingdom. While both siblings are awed into speechlessness when they see the princess, Klods-Hans charms her by turning a dead crow into a royal meal, a wooden shoe into a frying pan, and a handful of mud into a delicious sauce.

As we see it, the story teaches us an important lesson about circular economy. Not necessarily that dead crows, wooden clogs and a glob of mud should be seen as top-notch recyclable resources, but that by seeing treasures where others see waste, big victories are won. Although disrespected by his two self-confident brothers and mocked for going against the established norms, Klods-Hans surprised every-one and married the king's daughter. Thus, we learn that success de-pends on having courage when seeing possible failure and remaining steadfast when confronted with disdain and disapproval.

Klods-Hans was not just unique in his way of thinking; he also made sure that the most important stakeholder – the princess – would buy into his vision and see things from his perspective. Breaking with tradition and winning depended on having a coherent story and being able to communicate it in a clear and persuasive way. Af-ter all, if no customers are willing to listen to your pitch, your impact will – no matter how good your ideas are – be limited.

That's why we are writing this book, and why we set up the Wasteland Exhibition in different cities in Denmark and abroad: to show – in the best Klods-Hans style – how waste can become resources and be recycled as building materials. We do this with a genuine desire to make sustainability both understandable and appealing to people at large. To inspire them by demonstrating that we can do things differently.

Every day, we find inspiration from the fairy-tale of Klods-Hans. It is a narrative we turn to when trying to explain how circular innovations can thrive and ultimately achieve success.

One example of our respect for, and identification with, Klods-Hans can be seen in the beautiful interior cladding Lendager Group made for the office building "Copenhagen Towers II." The wooden panels are made of old window frames – in fact, the ugliest windows we could find – frames that nobody liked or could see any value in and were therefore ours to take, a project we won a Danish Design Award for in 2018.

That is the kind of experience we have built on and shared in order to encourage many more potential Klods-Hanses out there. Companies and politicians have recently begun to realise that sustainable businesses, with circular economy, benefit both the planet and their shareholders. But, all too often, the distance between the visionary idea and the measurable result is too big for even the most ambitious companies. That is where Klods-Hans and our methodology come in. We think the world needs more out-of-the-box thinkers like him.

The more we thought about this mythical anti-hero, the clearer it became that the relation between his story and ours goes much deeper than turning waste into gold. It's about celebrating diversity and about seeing flexibility and ingenuity as strengths. Thus, we at Lendager Group have now named a "Klods-Hans of the month" to honour the employee who has excelled at seeing possibilities rather than obstacles and achieved success by pursuing it step by step. In order to be a modern-day Klods-Hans, you must be willing to challenge convention and break the existing framework. Certainly, you

Designing for prosperity

have to see the barriers and the risks, but you can't accept them as roadblocks. On the contrary: In order for your business to succeed, you must identify the structures, rules and regulations that stand in your way in order to overcome them! Only then can you – with your unique idea that satisfies an unprecedented need – identify business opportunities, create sustainable change, and position yourself in an advantageous sweet spot with limited competition.

Cities of the future

"It is all too often forgotten that the whole point of a city is to bring people together, to facilitate interaction, and thereby to create ideas and wealth. To enhance innovative thinking and encourage entrepreneurship and cultural activity by taking advantage of the extraordinary opportunities that the diversity of a great city offers"

Geoffrey West - theoretical physicist

THE ROLE OF CITIES

The world is changing. But that's not a big surprise. It always has, and always will. *How* we react to these changes is what we should pay attention to. And what better way to do that than by thinking about the idea of the city. Because cities are indeed proof of mankind's greatest achievements – built, renovated and expanded when resources and the labor supply were seemingly infinite. A powerful demonstration of mankind's victorious domestication of nature. Old and natural has been replaced with new and artificial – and what used to be local is now global.

But the ever-increasing changes in demography and climate are now requiring us to revise our once-certain perceptions. Today, cities together with urban buildings and constructions are by far the largest single area where we face major challenges in terms of escalating resource consumption. The built environment in urban areas accounts for 39% of our total CO2-emissions[1]. A number that will grow significantly if we do not change our way of thinking about the role of the city and the escalating consumption of resources. Of course, we cannot just stop building cities and urban areas completely. Nor should we. By the year of 2050 we will be 9.8 billion people on Earth, and 68% of our global population will have settled in our fast-growing urban areas[2]. The global middle-class is also rising, with 160 million people making in into this socio-economic segment each year. This means that in a week from now, the Earth will be housing 1.5 million more people, the global-middle class will have grown larger by 3 million people, and another 3 million people will have moved from a rural to an urban life[3]. The UN-Habitat (United Nations Human Settlements Programme) estimates that 60% of the new urban areas needed in 2030 is yet to be built[4], while 75% of the needed infrastructure in 2050 is not in place either[5].

Changes are thus inevitable – the question is, how do we let them affect us. One ambitious attempt to take control of these changes and move them in the best possible direction was made by the United Nations in 2015. On September 25th of that year, world

1. UN environment, 2017. GLOBAL STATUS REPORT 2017: Towards a zero-emission, efficient, and resilient buildings and construction sector

2. UN Department of Economic and Social Affairs, 2018. World Urbanisation Prospects: The 2018 Revision

3. International organisation for Migration, 2015. World migration report 2015 – Migrants and Cities

4. Clos, J., 2016. The opportunity to build tomorrow's cities. World Economic Forum

5. World Economic Forum, 2018. Circular Economy in Cities: Evolving the model for a sustainable urban future

leaders adopted the sustainable development agenda, specifying 17 goals to ensure a cleaner, more equal, prosperous and balanced world community by the year 2030.

These Sustainable Development Goals (or SDGs) are already taking up a lot of space in the minds and bodies of companies, NGOs, and governments – and not least in the consultancies and special-interest groups all over the world.

But how do we make sure that by focusing on one SDG goal we do not compromise or neglect another? That, in fact, we not deliver just one SDG effectively, but all seventeen? Especially when it comes to the economically and ethnically complex city, where it has almost become the rule to give with one hand and take with the other? For example, how do we successfully achieve SDG 11 – ensuring "affordable housing for all" – while at the same time also meeting the objective of SDG 13 which addresses the need for climate action?

Our ambition for the built environment requires switching from a linear to a circular economy – thus significantly reducing CO2-emissions while catering to the rapid demand for new urban areas. To add value by doing much more with much less.

And why stop here? Imagine if buildings and cities could become the embodiment of the SDGs – where one goal does not impose restrictions on another, but puts them together and creates synergy in a common cause. That is not impossible. But it demands us to stop treating resources, buildings and cities as individual entities and start looking at them as parts of a greater system. With both eyes open, remember? Moving away from isolated perspectives and towards a more holistic view.

FROM A MECHANIC TO AN ORGANIC
UNDERSTANDING OF THE CITY

First thing we can start doing is to see the city as a living organism; much like how Alexander Von Humboldt rejected the notion of nature as a machine, and introduced a new understanding of Earth as one great living organism[6]. An organism connected through ecosystems influencing and determining one another's existence. Similarly, we should think of the built environment and cities in total as parts of a larger living organism. Because when we start seeing the bigger picture and begin connecting the dots – the citizens, the materials, the buildings, the districts, the cities, the nations, the regions, the world – then synergies will arise, and problems will become part of the solution. It is important to understand that if buildings and cities are to seize the potential and drive the transformation to mitigate climate change, they must have a greater purpose than themselves alone. If we are to succeed in creating a sustainable society, we must also create social cohesion. And not just any sort of social cohesion—but one that adds value to both the strong and the weak, making sure it's the highest common denominator that sets the standards. It is part of a regenerative society in which resources are not shared in a zero-sum game but are instead valued and circulated for all to prosper from.

In the next chapter, we explore what a regenerative city could look like and what global impact it could cause. But first allow us to explain why cities are the natural starting point for implementing solutions to the SDGs and what challenges they must overcome in order to succeed.

6. Wulf, A., 2015.
The Forgotten Father
of Environmentalism.
The Atlantic

Courtyard of the Future. Planning for future climate changes and Copenhagen's growing challenges with floods.

THE SYSTEMIC BEHAVIOUR OF CITIES

As of today, 54% of the world population are currently living in urban areas; accounting for 85% of the global GDP-generation according to a 2017 report on Circular Cities from The Ellen Macarthur Foundation and Google[7]. In the era of late modernity, cities have thus become the epicentre of both problems and opportunities for future prosperity and health of our planet and our growing population.

7. Ellen MacArthur Foundation, 2017. Cities in the circular economy: An initial exploration

According to the Circular Cities report, cities are the dominant "aggregators of materials and nutrients, accounting for 75% of natural resource consumption, 50% of global waste production, and 60-80% of greenhouse gas emissions." So, what should we do to prevent further massive environmental damage? Simply break up the cities and move towards a decentralised urban planning approach? Surely that is not the right way forward, and here is the reason why: *the city does not scale linearly.* As a matter of fact, when we scale cities we use less and get more. Sounds odd? Let's take a closer look at the facts and arguments. We are sorry for being so nerdy here, but we really want you to give you the entire picture.

The visionary physicist Geoffrey West has been collecting and analysing historical data on the development and growth of cities for most of his career. However, he begins from a very different starting point than most, as he starts by asking: "Could there conceivably be a few simple rules that all organisms obey, indeed all complex systems, from plants and animals to cities and companies?"[8] From this curiosity, he goes on to present empirical examples highlighting the existence of strong regularities in the data structures, all together suggesting a common conceptual framework that cities quantitatively scale with size. *A science of cities*, as he calls it.

8. West, G., 2017. Scale: The Universal Laws of Life and Death in Organisms, Cities and Companies

Breaking it down: it means that we experience a 25% discount on necessary inputs pr. citizen such as energy, water and raw materials with the doubling of the city's size.

West explains this as a result of the 'metabolism of the city' – under-stood as the biological process of energy transformation and waste-management in the cells of the living organisms[9].

9. The first notion of 'urban metabolism' goes all the way back to the 19th century when Marx and Engels made the first references to actual metabolism when discussing the relation between physical labour, natural resources and industrialisation.

And it gets even better. When we scale cities, not only do we get this 25 percent discount on input – we also evoke a 15 percent increase in the output of cities, including an upsurge in patents and innovations much needed to drive the necessary change towards a regenerative society. He also finds this systematic behaviour to be a global phenomenon, similar for all cities where data were obtained.

For a city to be regenerative, it needs to give back more than it takes. It is therefore a crucial factor that a city does not simply turn inwards – focusing solely on the well-being of the citizens within its geographical perimeter. Instead, it ought to seize the increased power which urbanisation and geopolitics in effect give the city. Simply put, the city now has the responsibility for our global well-being. It is necessary to ensure that the benefits created within the city not only benefit the city itself but global citizens at large.

URBANISATION, DEINDUSTRIALISATION AND THE RESTRUCTURING OF CITIES

While cities are great places for human ingenuity and the development of new ideas, changes in how we structure and treat our cities still need to take place. As we enter the fourth industrial revolution (see *Part IV* for more info on the 4IR), this is more apparent than ever. The first and second industrial revolutions brought about a series of dramatic and unpredictable events – leading to rapid changes in our planet's ecology, environment and climate over a short period of time. Spurred on by the invention of the steam engine, the discovery of electricity, the large-scale production of iron and steel, and the unlocking of energy-dense oil reserves, the juggernaut of modernity gained force[10]. People put rural and agrarian societies behind them in favour of an urban, industrial life, where mechanised mass production was made possible and labour demand rose quickly. Many of the underlying structures of life as we know it today came into place during this era and didn't really change much until the third revolution got underway in the 1980s. Since that time, digitalisation has quickly replaced our analogue systems and exponentially accelerated the

10. The notion of modernity as a juggernaut-like creature was coined by sociologist Anthony Giddens in his book "The Consequences of Modernity" from 1991.

latest wave of globalisation – and in many aspects, this digital revolution is still ongoing.

As West discovered, cities share similarities with other living organisms. But one radical difference stands out. Cities rarely die. In fact, they can continue to thrive not just for centuries but for millennia. This is also one major difference between cities and corporations; which unlike cities have a relatively short life-span and scale differently.

Cities have the privilege to run on a less top-down controlled framework and are divided by autonomous, diverse and multi-dimensional entities and sub-cultures. This, West thinks, result in the cities' outstanding resilience and open-ended growth and superlinear scaling. But are cities' future longevity then always assured? Even though people in general are taking root in urban areas to a still greater extend – the concept of urban depopulation where cities are shrinking has been a well-known phenomenon since the Second World War[11]. In an era of continuous deindustrialisation, automation and digitalisation – where jobs are moving from resource extraction and manufacturing to the service sectors – some cities are struggling to avoid becoming obsolete ghost towns. We've seen it everywhere from US cities such as Detroit, Flint and New Orleans to the North-eastern city in China, Yichun, where more than 100.000 people left the city between 2005 to 2015 due to excessive resource depletion in the area[12].

In total, these two simultaneous trends of rapid urbanisation and urban depopulation call for an increased emphasis on the need for urban development strategies that can make our cities even more agile, livable and forward-moving. We obviously cannot rely only on the cities' seemingly-innate ability to scale inputs and outputs alone. What really matters is what we scale, not just the rate at which we do it. Yes, we want exponential growth, but it has to be the right sort of growth. And this is where we humans become essential. Guiding the path, creating the innovations and designs that enable success. And our importance only increases as our global population grows.

In regard to the cities and the so-called "rust-belts" suffering from sudden industrial decline, we have to reinvent their focus and lively

11. Biswas A. et al., 2018. In an urbanizing world, shrinking cities are a forgotten problem. World Economic Forum

12. Allen, K., 2017. Shrinking cities: Population decline in the world's rust-belt areas. Financial Times

hood – opening both eyes and seeing the hidden resources and possibilities hitherto unimaginable for most of us. Imagine what we could do with the abandoned industrial complexes, the old shipyards, the laid-off infrastructures and many empty houses. What if we found a way to re-activate these left-overs that could help us lay the foundation for new communities – either at the same place or removed to somewhere else?

As we will demonstrate throughout the next cases and chapters, there are many ways to combine the challenges with growing and shrinking cities in a symbiosis – making sure both places get ready for the circular economy and become regenerative.

In some of the areas with urban depopulation, local entrepreneurs are now trying to replace fossil fuel jobs with jobs in the renewable energy sector by re-educating its workers and setting up locally funded solar and wind-power projects with big success.

This is just one example of by decoupling future economic growth from the excessive use of virgin materials – which so far has been an inevitable precondition for development – we can kickstart the development of new, regenerative societies.

All it takes is the combination of new ideas and a change of mind. So, let's take a better look at this change of mind and the transition towards producing positive energy instead of a negative footprint. It is time to explore what we believe is a replicable methodology of West's notion of urban metabolism – grounded in the principles of circular economy.

But first: a case about upcycling bricks, wood, and industrial elements in new houses.

A rendering of The Resource Rows with its upcycled brick facade.

THE RESOURCE ROWS

From abandoned buildings to thriving communities

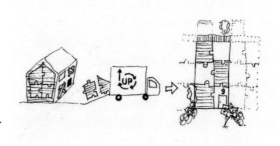

Upcycled wall elements form a piece of the puzzle of The Resource Rows.

Imagine a city defined by its abundance rather than its scarcity of resources. A city with a thriving, healthy population known for its world-class regenerative innovations, low level of socio-economic inequality, high sense of community, and unshakeable feeling of trust among its citizen. Delicious sustainable food is found on every street corner, and the air quality is the best among world capitals. Similarly, biodiversity, industry and the business community are all thriving on the 86.39 square kilometers that make up the city. It has often been called the happiest place on earth, but that's not really the point. The point is that it has become the first, regenerative, carbon-positive city in the world. Tell us, does this urban center sound like a utopia?

Let us quickly tell you it is not. With a little help, it can be very real. And how do we know that? Because we live in this city. Or, perhaps not entirely. But every day we work – little by little – to make sure that Copenhagen – our city – will become the city we dream about and just described. And every day we see tangible results of this coming true.

Then you might ask: Can other larger cities copy Copenhagen's model? Definitely. Especially when we look at a long string of global megatrends and leap-frogging technological progresses. Moreover, even though Copenhagen still has a long way to go before it finds truly sustainable ways to reduce waste production and CO2-emissions, we dare to believe. In fact, we have been hopeful for quite some time now, especially since we have already seen what is possible when we imagine a regenerative city enabled by circular economy.

As we are writing these pages, our colleagues are in the middle of completing The Resource Rows, a residential project in one of Copenhagen's new urban developments called Ørestad. The future inhabitants can look forward to living in a community of attractive, modern buildings. Buildings not made of virgin materials imported from afar, but of local resources normally considered nothing but useless waste. Due to a smart design phase, a fair amount of audacity and a lot of skilled local workers, we've managed to reactivate this so-called waste by transforming it into high quality and valuable building materials.

That was the idea of the Resource Rows from the beginning: to take something from the building industry with a perceived low value and prove it to be a treasured resource for a large group of people. Not just providing housing, but creating a healthy community based on core Danish values of sharing with each other, helping out one another and enjoying life together. Ideas taken from the traditional allotment associations that once were common in the outskirts of Copenhagen and very much have shaped the DNA of the now so famous notion of hygge. This is how we made it happen.

UPCYCLING WOOD – FROM SUBWAY TUNNELS TO BUILDING FACADES

Throughout Copenhagen, the current public-transportation system is expanding, making metropolitan travel even more efficient. In the making of the new tunnels, 900 tons larch wood was used in the transportation and construction of concrete tunnel elements for the new underground. Once at its destination, the wood was no longer needed. It thus, in a very short time, went from being a high-quality material to end-of-use waste, which the Metro company would have to pay to get rid of.

Luckily, we got hold of 300 tons of the wood before it was thrown out. So now, instead of being burned and down-cycled in a waste-to-heat process, the wood will be used to build beautiful facades, terraces, floors and balconies at the Resource Community, serving middle-class families of Copenhagen at a median price point. For all the wood used outdoors, we apply an old Japanese technique (Yakisugi) of charring the surface with fire to impregnate it – making it fire proof and resistant to fungus and insects (and fire, too) completely without using any chemicals.

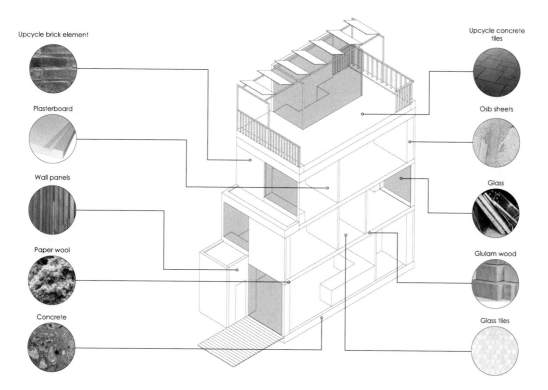

Upcycle brick element

Plasterboard

Wall panels

Paper wool

Concrete

Upcycle concrete tiles

Osb sheets

Glass

Glulam wood

Glass tiles

The Resource Rows uses what others might consider waste as valuable building materials, ready to be upcycled and re-designed.

The rooftop area on The Resource Rows will be giving space to 52 greenhouses - all supplied by collected rain water for irrigation.

Case 3: The Resource Rows

Case 3: The Resource Rows

THE RESOURCE ROWS
Type: Residential
Area: 9000 square metres
Site: Ørestad, Denmark
Client: NREP A/S and
Arkitektgruppen A/S
Contractor: Arkitektgruppen A/S
Engineer: MOE A/S
Architect: Lendager ARC
Status: Ongoing
Year: 2015 -
Partner in charge: Anders Lendager
Project leader: Jesper Høiberg
Team: Anette Orth Laybourn, Iben
Nørkjær, Torben Vestergaard,
Niklas Nolsøe, Sunniva Garshol,
Signe Balthazar Munk, Nicholas
Ransome, Mathias Ruø Rasmussen,
Kaare Karrebæk Thun

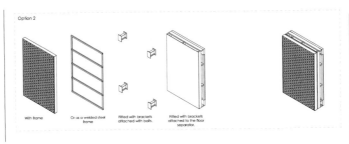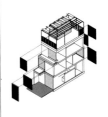

Option 2

With frame | Or as a welded steel frame | Fitted with brackets attached with bolts. | Fitted with brackets attached to the floor separator.

The elements and layers of the upcycled brick element wall.

A patchwork of upcycled brick walls coming to live in the construction of The Resource Rows.

STØDPUDELAGERET CARLSBERG BYEN | MATRIX CARLSBERG BYEN | AALBORG UNIVERSITET | TAP E CARLSBERG BYEN

The bricks are cut-outs from different buildings around Denmark – adding a history to the new dwellings and giving used materials new life.

Case 3: The Resource Rows

UPCYCLING BRICKS
– FROM OLD BREWERY TO
NEW DWELLING

Another important material in making the Resource Rows coming true is the re-use of bricks from old, abandoned buildings. De-industrialisation and urbanisation are two immense forces leaving a lot of old factories, warehouses and homes behind. This has made of wondering for a long time: how do we even out this transition from industry to service, from land to city, without losing valuable materials in the process? What if we could bring our houses, or part of our houses with us when we moved?

Once, we actually recycled old bricks. But since the 1960s, we invented a mortar so strong that the bricks are now breaking before the mortar does when trying to take them apart. So, we came up with a way to cut out brick-walls as whole modules rather than trying to use the individual brick one by one. While at the same time designing for circularity, making the brick-modules applicable as an aesthetically facade-element. And we are really proud of that, because recycling bricks matters. For every brick we give new life – we save ½ kilo CO2.

For the Resource Rows, we were able to re-use the bricks from the old iconic headquarters of the Danish brewery Carlsberg as well as from other abandoned houses and factories in Denmark. Instead of simply crushing the old brick walls and using it for road-fill, we bring the value and history of the used materials into a new, fresh community.

THE MAKING OF A COMMUNITY
– GREEN HOUSES, RAINWATER
COLLECTION AND SHARING

Speaking of community, you might wonder how the process of upcycling waste through the principles of circular economy can be worth more than just making the built environment more environmentally sustainable? Well, besides from mitigating climate change, the upcycled materials – if used properly – can also be a valuable resource in the making of a community. As mentioned, the tradition of allotment associations and the concept of sharing has been a core inspiration for this project.

The entire roof area on top of the Resource Rows will therefore be giving space to 52 greenhouses – made from upcycled window glass of course. Here, residents are given gardens tools to share for cultivating the green roof. If done successfully, they will be able to grow up to 4 tons of fruits and vegetables each year. Not just saving them money, but also reducing emissions from imported goods and providing a huge opportunity to be part of something; a community. To connect to two sides of the roof, an old industrial footbridge is going to run over the courtyard – giving the residents a chance to visit each other and see the whole community from above.

Other vital parts are water and energy, so we decided to make the Resource Rows able to collect sun and rainwater as well. The rainwater, perhaps more common in Copenhagen than sun at times, will thus help irrigating the green roof or flushing toilets in the many bathrooms. Finally, the underground parking area will be equipped with both bikes and electric cars to share amongst the residents.

Now. Keep in mind that we did all this without compromising on neither price, quality nor aesthetics of the building. At a cost-neutral price compared to any other benchmark building, we were able to challenge the issues of the built environment, food, water and energy – while also creating local jobs in the making.

This is just one example driven by individual passion and refusal to give up or give in. Imagine the possibilities if we combined global efforts and started working together across industries to accelerate and scale the journey towards regenerative buildings, communities and cities in harmony with nature? We can do it.

A SCIENCE OF CITIES
– FROM URBAN METABOLISM
TO REGENERATIVE CITIES

Having an infection in your little toe can cause a fever in your entire body. The reason? Your body is composed of trillions of interconnected parts, and what goes on in each and every intestinal one can influence our overall wellbeing, both physically and mentally. Similarly, what we put into our cities matters to the overall wellbeing of our society. China is, unfortunately, a great example of this. By responding to an exponentially increasing demand for energy by supplying coal power, the air of countless Chinese cities has become so polluted that the citizens' health is threatened[13].

Our cities – like our bodies – have a metabolism. But unfortunately we are not being very thoughtful about how we nourish them. This is the main reason why urbanisation is having such negative effects on our climate. But it does not have to be that way. Urbanisation and the built environment could play crucial roles in creating a sustainable world, rather than being main contributors to the problem.

Urban Metabolism can be a challenging concept, so allow us to explain our version. By seeing the city as a living organism, we can investigate how the different parts of the city's body are connected, and how vital they each are for the proper function of the whole. Therefore, we must pay attention to what we feed the "body" to ensure it is healthy and able to regenerate its cells. A so-called regenerative city.

So what nutrients do we feed our cities wi today and how effective are they? The conventional modern city consumes energy, water, virgin materials, land and people. As framed by the visionary American scientist Lewis Mumford: "The chief function of the city is to convert power into form, energy into culture, dead matter into the living symbols of art, biological reproduction into societal creativity."[14] However, the problem with today's cities is that most of these elements are leading to congestion or corrosion of the organism – one way or the other.

13. Air pollution in China is currently responsible for more than 1.5 million premature deaths a year, according to a report by the health effects institute (HEI).

14. This exception is from Mumford's famous book "The City in History" from 1961, in which he presents a theory for an organic city in balance with nature.

As seemingly harmless as these transformative functions of the city may sound, they are not without consequences. Burning fossil fuels leads to rising temperatures and climate change. Air pollution leads to lung and heart diseases. Water can cause both floods and droughts. Production and consumption lead to infinite amounts of waste and pollution and the contamination of oceans, soil and air. Claiming and transforming nature in order to create dense human settlements not only eliminates existing food sources, communities and renewable natural materials, it rapidly annihilates Earth's natural ecosystems that have been balancing the inputs and outputs of natural resources for eons.

Therefore, we need to fundamentally change how we plan, build and manage cities. We must reset the urban metabolism and its flows and reinvent a system in which cities and their inhabitants do not have to thrive at the expense of, but in harmony with nature. This is where the notion of circularity comes in handy.

To succeed with this transformation, we need to build on the theories and ideas of Geoffrey West, the British theoretical physicist, who developed a scientific model of cities, mapping the flows of inputs and outputs, and used the findings to systematically diminish the negative carbon footprint. Indeed, there is really no reason not to. But it is one thing to be mindful of a city's resource flow and its effects. It is another to make sure that we utilise the resources to their full extent, and at their highest value.

Somehow along the way, we stopped doing this. Instead, hyper confident after the go-go years of industrialisation, globalisation and innovation, we became careless with our production and consumption. We started seeing resources as abundant – even endless– and Earth as something that existed exclusively to serve our needs. "Industrialise or perish" was the motto we grew accustomed to during the millennia's mega-growth period, and so we did. But now it seems as if we might risk perish anyway because of this very imperative[15].

Our current system is not only destructive – it is also inefficient and irrational. While we have realised that virgin materials are

15. In Mahatma Gandhi's uproar against reckless industrialisation in India and around the world, he became known for the slogan: 'Industrialise, AND perish!' - arguing that instead of rapid urbanisation we ought to re-model our villages as healthy alternatives instead. This was back in 1945.

becoming scarce, the materials we have already extracted, used and thrown away have not, in fact, disappeared. Indeed, they are still accumulating, waiting to be put back into use again. We must start taking their true value seriously.

Moreover, as world population, urbanisation and prosperity are on the rise, we desperately need to reduce climate change and keep global warming in check. The key to getting our planet back on a restorative and regenerative track is to find new ways of enabling growth without emissions and the extraction of new raw materials.

This implies that growth is a part of the solution – though a different kind of growth than we are used to: A real, tangible growth that allows us to meet the needs of our global population and, most importantly, ensure that prosperity is equitably distributed. For this to become possible, the notion of "growth" is central. For the first time in history we can use growth as a positive influence on climate change, becoming a mitigating rather than an accelerating factor to climate change.

To us, the chief function of the city is to create the synergetic flows of resources and to ensuring that they work towards a prosperous future for all. In other words: Cities can help create regenerative and restorative societies. The notion of urban metabolism is nothing new – we've known about it for centuries. It just never occurred to us to connect this accumulated massive information to our planning of cities and urban areas. But we are drawing attention to the phenomenon because we genuinely believe that the scenario of a thriving city, giving back more than it takes as described in the beginning of this chapter, is not a utopian fantasy, but a well-documented and feasible development of our world's urban spaces – no matter if they are in Copenhagen, Beijing, Nairobi or New York.

FROM INDUSTRIAL WASTE
TO GREEN MIDDLE-CLASS DISTRICTS
AND CIRCULAR BUSINESS CLUSTERS

What input does a city need, what resources are available and how do we optimize synergies and usage? To answer these questions, we look at how the different "body-parts" of the city are connected and how each of them are vital to the survival of the city in its entirety. Furthermore, we are interested in what the city feeds on – so that it can stay healthy and able to regenerate. In this way we create regenerative and resilient buildings and cities. What we apply is the notion of urban metabolism and seek to understand a given city or a specific districts' relationship to its surroundings. Its history, demography, old and current industries and businesses, and local political ambitions. We map its resource flows and evaluate how material, environmental and socio-economic components interact within these systems.

This holistic approach and contextual analysis give us the right tools to identify and plan a sustainable development strategy, built around the districts own unique composition. It enables us to upcycle local waste-materials and to re-activate old constructions, districts and cultural artefacts in innovative ways. Cutting CO_2-emissions, protecting biodiversity, allowing cost-reductions and creating local jobs.

A few examples of this are the transformation of the Coal Crane Bridge in the Danish city of Aarhus; the development of Varvsstaden in Malmö, Sweden, and the creation of The Ressource City in Næstved, Denmark.

The Coal Crane: In the South Harbour of Aarhus, we are going to transform the old Coal Crane Bridge to a new, green pathway connecting the harbour area with the rest of the city. Once providing the city's Gasworks with coal, the crane and bridge are about to become Aarhus' own 'High Line' – a transformative concept know from both New York and Seoul where former railroads and highways have become recreational spaces elevated above the cities' heavy traffic. Besides from the bridge itself, the project In Aarhus' South Harbour includes the establishment of recycling stations, a park and large open square – altogether linking commercial buildings with social initiatives in the district.

Varvsstaden: During its heyday in the 1950s and 1960s, the shipyard in Malmö's western harbour was the world's biggest – employing more than 6000 workers. However, the oil-crisis in 1973 marked the decline of the shipyard which shut down completely in 1986 – leaving behind a huge industrial area in decay. It wasn't until 2001 Malmö municipality began the redevelopment of the west harbour area. This time, the district was going to take on a more sustainable profile, and when we entered the process in 2016 to help a private developer, it was to start transforming the southern part called Varvsstaden. In an area supposed to house more than 1500 new residents, we carried out an analysis based on the triple bottom-line framework of social, environmental and economic aspects[16] – mapping the area's biodiversity resources, social resources, energy resources, water resources and material resources. Based on this, we came up with an urban symbiosis strategy we named 'the loop' – making sure that local resources are kept at their highest value in metabolic flow.

Ressource City: In the Danish city of Næstved, the Maglemølle Paper Mill once stood out as the city's proud flagship company and driving force of growth, providing jobs to more than 2500 workers. From its peak in the 1930s, the industrial site went through some profitable decades until it started showing signs of crisis in the 1970s and closed its last facility in the 1992. For a long time, Maglemølle was a closed-off industrial area of 90.000 square metres put on hold and disconnected from the rest of the city. But in 2016 we began the development of Ressource City – an ambitious project transforming the old area into a green cluster of industrial symbiosis based on the principles of circular economy. First step was to remake the old power plant as a resource center and then reconnecting the site with the rest of town through new infrastructure. Making use of the existing materials and facilities – by splitting up the gigantic mass of buildings into smaller parts with more light and air – we save otherwise needed virgin materials and CO_2-emissions.

16. The 'Brundtland Report' from 1987 carried out by the World Commission on Environment and Development is the first to really articulate the idea of sustainable development; laying the foundation for the definition of a triple bottom line and further understandings of sustainability.

Figure 07: Material Harvesting in the Demolition Process

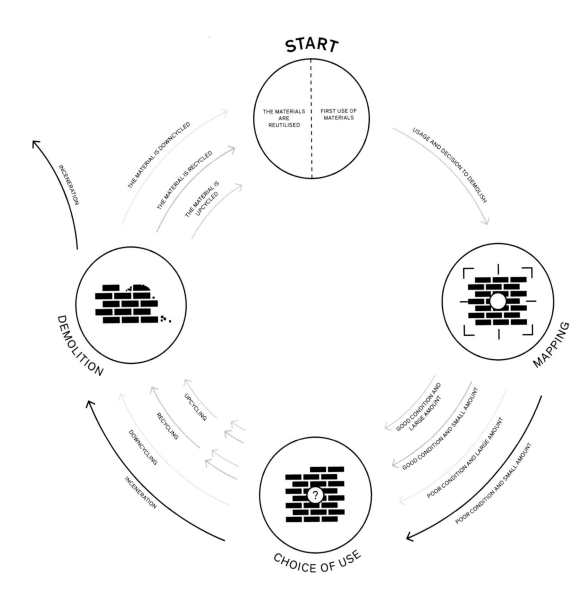

IT'S DOABLE:
THE STORY OF THE COPENHAGEN BIKES

To the moon and back – twice – or 33 times around the world. That's how much the citizens of Copenhagen bike in total… every day![17]

17. Astrup, S., 2016. Det cykler for København. Politiken

In fact, due to support from a broad coalition of politicians and public officials, they are using bikes more than cars, and the city has become globally renowned for its pro-cycling attitude. As a result, Copenhagen is a moonshot: "an idea so big, so bold, as to be impossible until it is not." Originally defined by John F. Kennedy, this is understood today as what the tech guys in the Silicon Valley series only dare to dream about.

The citizens of Copenhagen own 660,000 bikes – 6.6 times more than the total number of cars – and over the last twenty years bike traffic has increased by 68%, accounting for 45% of all trips to work or school, and more than a 4th of all families with children own a cargo-bike[18]. And don't be mistaken – biking in Copenhagen is far from a low-class phenomenon. People earning more than half a million DKK ($80.000) a year bike 29% more than those who earn half.

18. Cycling Embassy of Denmark, 2018. Facts about Cycling in Denmark

An international design magazine suggested that visitors to Copenhagen take a walk on the Knippelsbro Bridge and note the number of people on bicycles in defiance of the weather conditions as a tourist attraction. The city has 179 wet days per year, but rain or shine, wind, fog or snow, 31.620 cyclists crossing the bridge on a daily basis, simply because it is the easiest and most efficient transport modality. Indeed, for many years, the bike traffic on Knippelsbro bridge was even more hectic – up to 40.000 crossings every day – but as more bike-and-pedestrian designated bridges have appeared around the city, the system is rebalancing the traffic load as people migrate to quicker routes.

Over the years, the Copenhagen municipality has prioritised the construction of bike paths over roads and parking areas, since 2005, for example, it has spent 1 billion DKK ($160m) expanding the cycling infrastructure with new bridges, tracks and renovations aimed at "softer" transport modes[19].

19. Cathcart-Keays, A., 2016. Two-wheel takeover: bikes outnumber cars for the first time in Copenhagen, The Guardian

Cykelslangen (The Bicycle Snake) in Copenhagen has more than 14.000 daily users who altogether save time worth 800.000 USD annually. Developed by Dissing + Weitling Architects. Photo by Rasmus Hjortshøj — COAST Studio.

Not only do these physical upgrades make a big difference in the everyday life of Copenhagen's citizens, but the strategic political investment in making the city the world's biking capital has also yielded significant benefits.

First off, bike-riding has had a measurable effect on the environment. helping the city save 90.000 tons of CO_2-emissions annually[20]. Continuing the plan to increase bike traffic is a big part of Copenhagen's ambition to become the world's first carbon-neutral city. Besides these obvious CO_2- reduction results, supporting a city of pedalling habitants has helped the city reap significant health benefits.

20. Cycling Embassy of Denmark, 2015. Our daily bike rides benefit the climate immensely

When Copenhageners jump on their bikes instead of into their cars to go to work, school, yoga or the supermarket, they are helping to create a more sustainable, lovable and liveable urban area, with lower noise levels, as well as a lower mortality rate by almost 40%.[21] A new study in Denmark shows that if we Danes increase our biking with 10% - we can save 267,000 sick-days a year and generate an extra $160 billion for society each year. In fact, for every kilometre a bicycle rider pedals, society gains the equivalent of 18¢, whereas every kilometre an automobile driver travels results in a loss of 17¢.[22]

21. Murnane, K., 2017. New Research Indicates Cycling To Work Has Extraordinary Health Benefits. Forbes

22.1. Ritzau, 2018. Ny analyse viser den økonomiske gevinst ved cykling. Politiken Byrum

22.2. Schiller, B., 2015. How Copenhagen Became A Cycling Paradise By Considering The Full Cost Of Cars. Fast Company

In the Capital Region of Denmark, which has a population of 1.8 million people, the biking culture prevents at least a million days of sick leave every year – contributing positively to the bottom lines of both the public and the private sector.

Furthermore, Copenhagen's bike strategy of decoupling transportation from CO_2-emissions has been indispensable in branding it as a modern, health-conscious city that people want to both live in and visit attracting both talent and investments. In a recent analysis about tourism in Denmark conducted by Wonderful Copenhagen, 52% of the respondents reported that biking was one of their three main reasons for choosing Copenhagen as a destination.

The efforts to encourage bicycle riding have made the municipality a global case study for city planners and policy-makers. Every year, some 60 international delegations visit the city to gain know-how and inspiration from its successful theory of change.

This megatrend – often called Copenhagenization –testifies to the need to increase global population growth and encourage the rise of the middle-class, while simultaneously fighting climate change, pollution, obesity and time-consuming traffic congestions. Indeed, a report from 2011 concluded that, if all EU countries adopted a cycling pattern similar to Copenhagen's, the greenhouse-gas emissions from transportation could be reduced by up to 26%[23]. A prediction that deserves to be taken seriously.

23. Walker, P., 2011. Cycle like the Danes to cut carbon emissions, says study. The Guardian

The role of business

"The test of first rate intelligence is the ability to hold two opposite ideas in the mind at the same time, and still retain the ability to function. One should for example be able to see that things are hopeless and yet be determined to make them otherwise"

F. Scott Fitzgerald, The Crack Up, 1936

REWRITING THE HISTORY
OF GROWTH

As we have discovered throughout the book, there is a great potential for businesses in working with sustainability as a strategic growth driver. And that is pretty lucky for all of us, to say the least. Because we need you. The entrepreneur, the shop owner, the CEO of an SME, the product developer, the purchase manager, the analyst, the creative director, the craftswoman – all of you. We need businesses to lead the change by creating innovations that show the public and not least the politicians that changing the game is doable.

Why do we *need* to change the game and achieve systemic change? In short, because we have privatised all benefits but socialised all costs of pollution and emissions. As we mention earlier, putting a price on externalities is a great starting point to fixing this, but that alone won't take us all the way. We need to be mindful of the structures in society – the culture and mind-set that we have spent years building – and the need to break the harmful ones down in order to change our habits and behaviour. And more than anything, we need new ways of doing things. New innovations that enable prosperity for all without compromising our climate.

This also means that 'doing less bad' or being the leader within an industry is not enough. Admirable as it may be, it is not enough. Neither for society nor for your business, especially not if you wish to gain or maintain a competitive edge. Because it is only when sustainability becomes your core business, when you use it to increase the value you give to your clients and users that you will make a real change and gain that competitive edge.

In short: the bigger the impact the better the business.

DO OR DIE

We established Lendager TWC (The Circular Way) to help business-es gear up for the 4th industrial revolution and the current global trends by utilising a cross-disciplinary fundament. This helps us identify sustainable potentials for companies, public administrations and other organisations, as well as to offer practical solutions to the challenges that each assignment offers. Our purpose is to spear-head the creation of a regenerative society for all to thrive in by ena-bling business and climate to be each other's prerequisites through circular economy. In this section, we will share our experience and describe the tools we use to make this happen both within Lendager Group and externally.

It is no coincidence that our starting point, and what unites us as a business, is our vision and a collective answer to the question *Why?* Starting with the idea that we have seen an opportunity that most others have yet to experience. If you have that opportuni-ty, don't let yourself be brought down by the lack of equipment, financing, know-how etc. Instead, use the fact that so far you have dared to trust your vision and intuition and have had the courage to go your own way. You must continue to follow those instincts. Remember that the only constant is change. In a world where traditional market segments are becoming blurred, where limits are constantly broken, and technology develops at unprecedented speed, the ability to look beyond norms and to ask questions is essential.

We believe that growth and development are powerful enablers of change. Just as it has always been in nature. But this is only true if we make sure that the growth we hope to create is a means to an end – and not an end in itself.

"We cannot predict the future, but we can invent it,' as Dennis Gabor, Nobel Prize winner in physics, elegantly expressed it back in 1963, a quote that has since been rephrased by many. Among them Peter Diamandis, co-founder of the Silicon Valley institution Singularity University, who put it as, "The best way to predict the future is to create it yourself." Above all this means using strategy as an active – not a reactive – tool. Like Thomas Edison, Steve Jobs and others, you can create your market yourself. You do not have to blindly follow the rules of the current market and the economic macro trends that affect it. As you might have gathered by now, we believe that the circular economy is the right way forward. Which is why we created three tools to help unlock the potential: our *activity wheel*; our *circular opportunity tool*; as well as our extension of Ostwalder's *"Business model canvas."*

While the activity wheel and the circular opportunity tool can alert us to new opportunities for regenerative business through circular economy, the *business model canvas – the circular way* – enables a deep dive into the business-model potential and the risks associated with it. (Don't worry. We will describe all these tools and how you can use them later in this section).

Essentially, success still very much depends on the ability to innovate and create strategies around innovation and to continually deliver an edge with regard to value. In the next section, we will explain a bit more about the importance of *value* in order to future-proof both your business and the planet.

Figure 08: Three types of businesses:
The regenerative business, the responsible business
and the stranded business

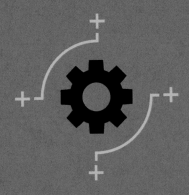

THE CIRCULAR INNOVATION

The current, linear system of limited resources and opportunities that exist today will strait-jacket your operations, preventing you from making a positive change. From our perspective, it is as simple as that. With circular economy we change the game radically and pave the way for a new vision where current obstacles are future opportunities. The tool to value innovation in the future is circular economy.

Given the direction our world and climate are moving, we believe the only way forward, the only way to create value as a business, is to decouple value from the use of materialisation and energy. That is, to move beyond a benchmark approach of doing "less bad." In that sense, we see three types of businesses:

1.   **The regenerative business**, where the business-model, use of materials and products enable the business and environment to be mutually beneficial.

2.   **The responsible business**, which is trying hard to do less bad, but still operates within a linear business model, making it difficult to decouple its growth and value from CO_2-emissions and the use of virgin materials.

3.   **The stranded business**, which has not yet had the need or the opportunity to operate differently. Instead, it is stuck in a traditional structure where business and environment are still each other's worst enemies.

What we will focus on here is how to become a regenerative business. By which we mean a business that achieves value innovation by combining innovation with circular economy and design-thinking. Mixing these three elements will create the pathway for you to transform and grow your business sustainably. We call it "the Circular Way of Value Innovation".

But, first, some definition of terms.

CIRCULAR ECONOMY
Has traditionally been described as the process of decoupling growth from materialisation. We propose a changed focus, expressed as the process of decoupling value from materialisation, which focuses on quality rather than quantity, and content over numbers. The question is, how can we increase value to ensure liveability and prosperity for our global population?

VALUE INNOVATION
Is about more than just innovation. Without it, a company is caught in a trap where products only develop gradually to keep up with the competition. As value for the buyer is measured by the usefulness and price of the company, and value for the company is based on price and cost-structures – value innovation is only achieved when the whole system of a company's usefulness, price and cost-activities are aligned.

Building on that, we propose an add-on: making it possible to dissociate value from materialisation, energy consumption and emissions. If you are an innovator, it is not enough to focus solely on the value delivered to the individual buyer (although value is still very relevant). Instead, you must take it even further and focus not just on the added value benefitting the buyer *but also on the value enabled by circular economy to society as a whole.*

When we say, "enabled by circular economy," we mean to highlight the opportunity *to see the circular economy framework as a toolbox.* A toolbox to change the rules of the game – making sure that our resources are utilised at their highest value and that business, people and planet are aligned. A great way to achieve value innovation is by resource optimisation, where the creation of value becomes possible without the need for new virgin resources or, as we will see, the design of new materials, products and business models that decouple value from the use of materials and emissions.

What the *Circular Opportunity Tool* visualises is the sweet spot between the cost of the innovation and the value that it gives the buyer. What makes it different from traditional strategy and so very useful for circular economy is the fact that it challenges the status quo. It does so by ignoring the traditional either/or thinking, where you have to choose between a strategy of either cost-cutting (by offering a lower price) or product differentiation (by creating a premium product). The aim is to create innovations that make both strategies available at the same time – in other words, offering better quality at a lower price.

DESIGN (THINKING)

Here, design serves as the key to success and forward momentum. It ensures that we can create innovations where value is decoupled from materialisation and CO_2-emissions without compromising on price, aesthetics or quality. We use design-thinking as the primary tool for opening our eyes wide, enabling us to see opportunity where others see constraints.

Sometimes visionary pioneers of circular economy experience what we call an "a-ha moment," that is, the realisation that a good idea or even a great invention is not enough. You might create an invention, but if you fail to see how it could become commercially viable, it's not worth much, since impact lies in implementation at scale.

Instead, the value a product creates should correlate with the costs that the users and the market are willing to pay. It might not be the traditional market or users, but at the end of the day, someone must be willing to pay. This may seem obvious, but we have experience with way too many great inventions and ideas that aren't thriving due to the fact that their creators have – although admirably – only been focusing on solving global problems.

We need those inventions more than anything, but we also need them to be put into use on a grand scale—that is where the notion of value comes into play. Therefore, a key take-away is *the combination of innovation and strategy in order to achieve value.*

What we want to provide here is the assurance that not only will there be a planet for people to prosper on in the future, but also that sustainable business will have a prosperous future and will be incentivised to keep on the trajectory of creating a regenerative society for all to thrive in.

Simply put, we want to future-proof business and the planet.

It is important to stress that, for us, this is not a matter of either/or – business or planet – but the combination that creates the solution. And that's what we mean when we talk about "prerequisite" – the certainty that, in order to secure business, we need to protect the environment, and vice versa. Our ambition is not just to solve one problem, but several problems at the same time.

For example, just as you can't merely include sustainability in your business plan as an unintegrated add-on – at least not without being willing to have it as an additional cost rather than a value add on. For sustainability to reap the benefits, you must strategically integrate it at the core of your business.

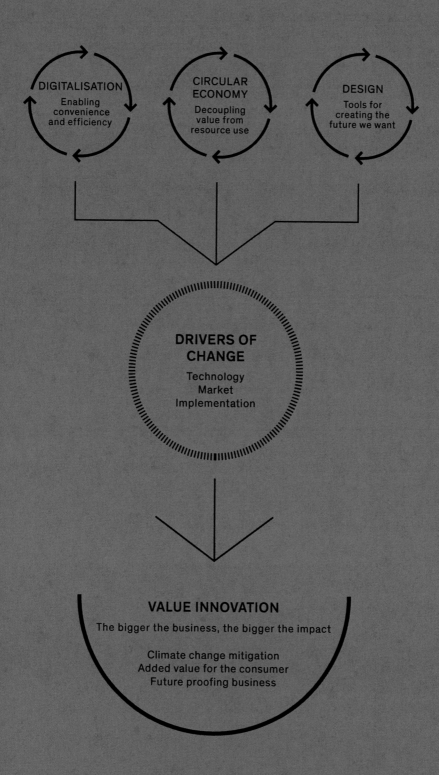

THE CIRCULAR WAY

As you have surely gathered by now, we are convinced that the best chance of achieving success in transitioning to a regenerative society, especially doing so in a timely way, is to connect business and environment in a synergetic manner. But there is no value innovation without a market for it, and no real circular economy without viable circular-economy business models.

For a business model to be circular it must – in its core – decouple value and growth from emissions and the use of virgin materials. A circular-economy business model thus produces value by fostering the regeneration of finite natural resources, while also striving to maintain the highest value and functionality of materials, products or components for as long as possible.

What follows is a comprehensive overview of a typical circular-economy business model, which we have divided into six subthemes:

1.   **Data.** As we are going to explain more thoroughly in the next chapter, big data and digitalisation have the potential to help us accelerate other circular-economy business models. This is based on the prospect of creating more transparent supply-chains and having a better understanding of resource-flows, consumer behaviour and product availability.

2.   **Resource recovery.** Enables a company to eliminate material leakage and maximise the economic value of product return flows and to make a business out of providing others with fully renewable, recyclable or biodegradable resource inputs that underpin circular production and consumption systems.

3.   **Take-back systems.** As the name indicates, this is about extending the life of your products and assuming responsibility for them and their materials by taking them back in various ways. By systematically doing so, and reusing products, components or materials in your own value-chain or by passing them on to others, you have gained an outstanding opportu-

nity to increase customer loyalty and create new sales-channels and side-business activities.

4.   **Circular supplies.** It is essential to establish a high-quality circular supply chain. One goal is to replace all new or virgin materials with fully renewable and recyclable resources. Other goals are to eliminate waste generation and to reduce the general material usage, decreasing the total input in your production no matter whether it consists of new or reused resources.

5.   **Product-service.** This is about providing new alternatives to the traditional model of "buy and own." Instead of focusing on the product itself, we look at their functions, and what people actually need. For example. people don't need lamps but light; they don't need cars but transportation options, and so on. Products are then used by one or many customers through a lease or pay-for-use arrangement.

6.   **Sharing.** Sharing is caring, to use an old cliché. By developing platforms for collaboration among product users, either individuals or organisations, we can utilise already-existing products and materials much more efficiently. The digital revolution became effective here – as apps and social media connects people and units better than ever.

In essence, these circular business models and activities are not so much about helping a company do just "a little less bad" than its competitors and be what one might call eco-efficient. Rather, these models are for an ambitious company that wants to reach for the stars and move towards becoming regenerative, giving more than it takes.

DEVELOPING A NEW INNOVATION
OR BUSINESS MODEL?

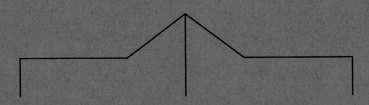

MARKET	TECHNOLOGY	IMPLEMENTATION
Assess the following:	Assess the following:	Assess the following:
1. Design and trend forecasting 2. Regulations 3. Supply & demand 4. Potential sales channels 5. Benchmarking	1. Design 2. Available technology 3. Supply-chain partners 4. Cost estimates 5. Environmental impact	1. Regulations 2. Supply & demand 3. Potential sales channels 4. Benchmarking

Output:	Output:	Output:
1. Design brief 2. Business case 3. Local business intelligence (BI) and testing partners	1. Product specification 2. Preferred production partner(s) 3. Value chain design	1. Launch plan 2. Preferred license partners 3. Risk assessment

Is it **desirable**? Is it **feasible**? Is it **viable**?

TECHNOLOGY – FRIEND OR FOE FOR A REGENERATIVE WORLD?

Right now, we have an unprecedented chance to scale circular-economy-based business models more quickly and more widely, thanks to the rapid technological developments. But the opportunity also comes with risk.

While more businesses are starting to seize the advantages enabled by circular economy, digitalisation and the new technological revolution are simultaneously moving forward at an increasingly fast pace. In fact, they have already paved the way for what we now see as the early stage of a 4th industrial revolution of smart technologies led by Artificial Intelligence (AI) and the Internet of Things (IoT) among others. And although it might seem unthinkable, the changes will take place at a constantly increasing speed. This in turn will make sustainability through circular economy even more necessary. On one hand, the technological progress is a necessary enabler for scaling circular economy. On the other, it is the primary reason why the shift from a linear to a circular economy is so timely.

How is that possible? Well, just like many other notoriously great inventions, technology in general has an enormous power to change the world for good. But, depending on how this power is channelled, the result can potentially also turn out to be horrific. Technological development gives us the chance to speed up the implementation of sustainable solutions. Yet this positive outcome depends, first, on whether we consciously choose to use technology in the right way and, second, on whether we have the proper systems in place to do so. If we do not, the development risks becoming a runaway train (with us on board) heading off the cliff. As environmental decay will just accelerate, as will the negative consequences of climate change.

As we have mentioned before, we are facing a rapid demographic change, including an increase in the global population as well as in the middle class, which will entail an increasing demand for basic goods, housing and transportation.

The million-dollar question is: how are we going to meet this demand? We know that centuries of mechanisation, mass production and automation have not only met our needs and brought radical improvements of life for billions of people. They have also wreaked havoc on our environment and put our climate under immense stress. Every year millions of tons of plastic end up in our oceans. Temperatures are rising, and the resources we have been using so lavishly to pay for our mass consumption are becoming scarce. The story of modernisation is the perfect example of how, thus far, the technological revolution has had a huge downside.

Fortunately, with the widespread ratification of the Paris Agreement in 2015 and collaboration by the international community to implement the UN Sustainable Development Goals, sustainability has become an important part of the global agenda.

While resources are dwindling, we have also developed innovations that were unimaginable just thirty years ago. The 4th industrial revolution has been responsible for a paradigm shift characterised by new technologies that blur the lines between the physical, digital and biological realms. Digital technology — such as artificial intelligence (AI), Blockchain, 3D printing and Internet of Things (IoT)— has had an astounding impact on the way we interact with one other and with our surroundings. Moreover, it has the potential to create a source of new value for society and an opportunity for businesses to replace our current "make, use, dispose" kind of linear economy and help redefine production and consumption in the 21st century. What do we mean by that? The best way to explain it is to share a few of the opportunities we are most excited about:

1.   **Blockchain** enables greater transparency, enhanced security and improved traceability, which provide the necessary trust and transparency to scale resource sharing and circulation. If we are to increase the sharing and circulation of resources on a business-to-business level as well as between individual users, transparency is essential. Blockchain technology provides just that: the opportunity to build global, decentralised trust. Whether it is a public Blockchain for resource sharing or a private Blockchain circulating a particular resource within a value

chain, it has become a lot easier to circulate resources. Thus, we can design the best global value chains for keeping resources in circulation and upcycle what has otherwise been deemed as waste.

2.   **Artificial Intelligence (AI)** provides the overview for waste to become resource. Imagine that, within milliseconds, you could determine the potential value of a waste resource if upcycled or, better yet, make sure that it was always upcycled at the highest value possible. Instantly making value and profit of turning waste into resource visible. Artificial intelligence provides the opportunity to quickly close the funding gap between the cost of collecting and processing the waste and the profit of the end resource. Artificial Intelligence allows us to analyse data with higher accuracy, increases resource efficiency and productivity, enables predictive maintenance and will open up further untapped potentials.

3.   **Internet of Things (IoT)**, will intensify connectivity between units and increase the performance of the circular economy. In terms of connectivity, humans have long been outcompeted by machines. 10 billion physical devices are connected through the Internet of Things (IoT) already and this number might grow to almost 50 billion by 2050[1]. As this huge inter-network is getting bigger, devices are constantly collecting and exchanging data about location, condition and availability of our resources. This will open for the implementation of "smart" energy systems and infrastructure in cities allowing us to adjust, reduce, streamline and automate our resource flows and consumption patterns.

1. Ellen MacArthur Foundation, 2016. Intelligent Assets: Unlocking the circular economy potential

4.   **3D Printing** – a paradigm-changing technology. Imagine if you could grind down your old garden furniture at your local 3D-printing centre and produce a new, fresh design from the old material in less than a couple of hours. 3D-printing is an additive manufacturing technique with the potential to distort the industrial landscape fundamentally, for good. 3D-printing allows us to design for circularity, achieve new forms and shapes and mass-customise these, to redesign, repair and remanufacture products – all through a technique widely driven by local, sustainable resources and available to the wider public and entrepreneurs.

5.   **Data collection**, the ability to collect and interpret data about the flow and traceability of resources, is a central factor in creating value in the interface of circular economy and digital solutions. The relevant data-points typically cover user habits (i.e. the type and quantity of waste, the type and amount of food purchases) or product lifecycle data (i.e. origin, lifecycle stages of every component of a product to better determine end of life time). Collecting this type of data can improve the circularity of the business , since the more knowledge it acquires about how the product or service is used, how much it is used, where it has previously been used and where it goes next, and how customers have responded, the easier it becomes to optimise its use. Hence, it essentially improves the circularity of the business.

But as data has become an increasingly powerful commodity, it becomes more challenging to establish ownership of and access to data as well. To build circular economy business models based on data, the business must either buy the necessary data or collect it themselves – a potentially time-consuming and resource -intensive process.

To sum up: Thanks to the technological develpoment, we now have an unprecedented opportunity to scale circular economy-based business models to larger audiences at a much faster pace than ever before. But the gain also entails risks, and we need to act quickly and start utilising the technological advancements for good.

"It's not the strongest of the species that survives, nor the most intelligent, but the one most responsive to change"

Leon C. Megginson – professor of Management and Marketing[2]

UNLEASHING THE POTENTIAL OF
CIRCULAR ECONOMY IN THE INFORMATION AGE

The relation between circular economy and technology is still in its initial phases, both fields are still maturing, and their potentials are yet to be fully discovered. With circular economy's strengths in increasing resource productivity, value retention and reduction in CO_2-emissions, together with digitalisation's ability to enhance transparency, efficiency and convenience and accelerate both pace and scale, the combination shows great potentials. But bridging the gap between the two fields might be easier said than done.

To some business leaders the combination can seem too complex. To others, these complications stand as great challenges as well as grand opportunities. With circular economy and technology as levers for systems change, the time to think big, act fast and make innovation a reality is now.

As we enter the 4th industrial revolution, our lives are about to be transformed again . At the core of this development lies global connectivity through digitalisation: the connection between human and human, human and machine, and, not least, between machine and machine. While the previous industrial revolutions have mostly empowered companies accelerating the unsustainable linear economy, this new wave of technology holds the key to a rapid transition to the circular economy. Technology cannot only scale and replicate; it can also empower consumers and communities, giving everyone a voice.

As every part of our lives from our buildings, our bodies to our brains are becoming increasingly integrated and extended by digital assets such as Blockchain, Internet of Things, and Artificial Intelligence etc. we have a golden opportunity to reinvent our relation to natural resources. Through the use of Internet of Things, we will intensify connectivity between units, gather data across things and people. Blockchain enables greater transparency, enhanced security and improved traceability. Artificial Intelligence allows us to analyse data with higher accuracy, increases resource efficiency and productivity, enables predictive maintenance and will open up further untapped potentials and 3D printing enabling local to be global. Just to name a

2. The quote comes from a speech that professor Megginson gave in 1963 at the convention of the Southwestern Social Science Association, in which he interprets the central ideas in Darwin's book 'the origin of the species'.

few of the possible positive outcomes.

To unlock the tremendous opportunities circular economy holds, it is critical to gain information about resource usage along the entire product lifecycle and every step of the value chain as well as information about material specifications for products. Doing so enhances value retention in every decision we make about design, manufacturing, and marketing. Technology is the key to unlocking this potential.

In the field of circular economy, value is created by extending the life of the product, maximising the utilisation of an asset, and creating one or multiple loops for the product's components and materials. Digital solutions provide value through gathering data about an item's location, condition and availability; by easing access to products and services; increasing traceability of materials; and making processes more convenient and efficient. The interface of circular economy and digital solutions thus provides a fertile ground for innovation and value retention.

Separately, circular economy and technology each represents new paradigms of producing, consuming and living. The interplay between the two will change the nature of human behaviour and will present a significant opportunity for almost every part of society.

If we grasp the potential that the circular-economy business models hold, we can cut the emission of 296 million tons of CO2 per year in Europe alone[3]. The new digital opportunities are already helping take the circular economy from a manual and sometimes-slow process, to one that is accelerated, streamlined, and efficient. Creating new circular resource-flows and consumption patterns which will extend a product's life-cycle while cutting its CO2-emissions – is essential to developing the future of industry and society.

3. Material Economics, 2018. The circular economy – a powerful force for climate mitigation

Tremendous potentials exist in the interface of technology and circular economy, and we must press on to unlock them as tools to mitigate climate change. If we do not, we risk the opposite effect.

KEY LEARNINGS

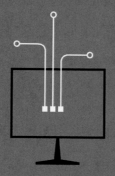

TECHNOLOGY

1. It is often not the technology itself that makes the business innovative and revolutionises their product or service, but rather how it is incorporated into the business model.
2. Businesses need data to truly unlock the potential for value creation their business model holds.
3. The data is there. Ownership and lack of incentive to share data limits start-ups' access to valuable data.

MARKET

1. Digital solutions can make it easier and more convenient for customers to go circular.
2. The digital solutions that connect the customer with the business need to be intuitive and accessible. If the interface between the customer and business is easy to implement and user-friendly, there is a better chance of getting customers onboard.
3. Applying digital solutions can potentially be the key to achieving competitive prices, quality and efficiency.

SKILLS & KNOWLEDGE

1. There are a lot of skills and knowledge available but finding the right interdisciplinary mix can be challenging.

GLOBAL PARTNERSHIPS
FOR ACCELERATING
THE CIRCULAR ECONOMY

"Strengthen the means of implementation and revitalise the global partnership for sustainable development", as states in the last UN Sustainable Development Goal - SDG 17. As such, it is a goal much unlike the other sixteen SDGs. While these goals dive into specific issues such as water, food, production etc., and articulate clear end-goals for what we need to accomplish in order achieve a sustainable world, the SDG 17 tells another story. The story of how we get there; through partnerships.

We could not agree more with the message of SDG 17. In a world of continuously increased complexity and accelerated pace, we need partnerships to ensure organisational agility as well as the necessary power to tackle the grand challenges we are facing. Therefore, we are thrilled that Kate Daly accepted our invitation to collaborate on a conversation chapter about partnerships and how to achieve circular value innovation through them. For after all - what better way to explore the opportunities for partnerships than through a partnership?

Kate Daly is the Executive Director of the Center for the Circular Economy at Closed Loop Partners, and one of Ditte's favorite go-to persons to discuss circularity and the transition towards a sustainable economy.

> **Ditte (D):** Kate, first of all thank you so much for participating and sharing your knowledge. Let's dive right into it. What drivers for circular economy do you see right now?

Kate (K): I see a lot of things happening. In the U.S. the transformation is very much driven by business interests rather than being driven by national regulation. Some of this work has been underway for decades and is driven by efficiency and cost-cutting goals; for example, the U.S. automobile industry has invested for years in remanufacturing. And now we're seeing global brands across sectors responding to emerging trends, both regulatory and social, in Europe and other parts of the world, by identifying the risks of business as usual and bringing this to bear in their U.S. markets. This makes sense, because the unintended consequences of our linear economy are already quite costly. Business and investors are beginning to recognise the need to transition from a linear perspective of risk to one that incorporates externalities, like supply chain disruption, market shifts from ownership to leasing that will impact traditional sales, the power of stakeholder activism, and the global impact of regional policy enactment, like the European Commission's proposal to ban single-use plastics and require producers to help pay for waste management and clean-up. I think businesses are starting to see impacts in other less obvious areas as well, for example talent retention. The growing millennial workforce is demanding purpose in their work, and businesses that incorporate a mission-driven ethos into their bottom line have a competitive advantage in talent attraction and retention. Consumers are exercising their power as well. Just a few examples: we're seeing an increase in shareholder activism in the U.S. on issues like single-use plastics, growing consumer interest in innovative new models for borrowing rather than owning, and increased focus on sustainability issues within fashion. Social media has played a big role, and in particular the impact of ocean plastics on marine life has really resonated. It's remarkable how influential viral videos of plastic-covered beaches and injured sea turtles and other marine life can be. This recognition that when we throw something away it doesn't just disappear is critical if we're to generate support in the U.S. for the broader systems change needed to transition to a circular economy, in the absence of national regulation or funding.

> D: For us, the goal is to combine circular economy, design thinking and innovation to deliver value innovation benefitting both people, profit and planet. What do you think are the most important factors if we are to be successful at creating the circular value innovation?

K: In order to reach the stage of "value innovation" there needs to be global recognition among competing businesses that opportunities for collaboration create value that outweighs the risks. The individual, brilliant product design is not enough. We must also factor in how the products or materials can retain their value at every stage of their life cycle, and this is only possible if the product is aligned with the infrastructure built to manage its recovery and reuse. When businesses collaborate to ensure access to post-consumer feedstocks, they can capture value for their own brand while fostering systems change across the value chain. The infrastructure, whether textile sorters, material recovery facilities or composting facilities, requires stable flows of materials and profitable market demand. Precompetitive partnerships are not only necessary to support this system but also profitable as the increased scale resulting from a unified materials flow drives down cost and future-proofs business investments.

The Closed Loop Fund is a great example of this concept in action. The Fund brings together the world's largest retailers and consumer goods companies, like Unilever, Proctor & Gamble, Coca-Cola and Pepsi, in a pre-competitive, collaborative investment partnership. The Fund invests in recycling infrastructure and technology to ensure a flow of recycled materials, so companies can manufacture at a lower cost and reduce reliance on raw materials. Municipalities are also the beneficiaries since expanded infrastructure reduces disposal costs and creates local jobs. We've seen growing interest in this model, and over the past three years the Fund has attracted nearly $100 million in co-investment and generated over $15 million in local economic benefit. The impact is straightforward: for every $1 invested, the Fund investment portfolio will return 220 pounds of recyclables to the supply chain and reduce or avoid 654 pounds of GHG emissions by 2025.

> D: Great, indeed a good example of the fact that circular economy is good not only for the environment but for business, jobs and society in general as well.
>
> Speaking of future-proofing businesses, where do you see the biggest opportunities for commercialising sustainable innovations at scale?

K: When thinking about design innovation, pre-competitive global partnerships are key, but another important approach is to rethink the design and reconsider the product from the very beginning. One recent innovation brought to market by Starbucks is a good example. They now offer a cold beverage cup redesigned with an attached spout rather than a separate straw. This solves for the challenge of plastic straws, which are not recyclable, while still delivering the iced drink in a format acceptable to customers. By focusing on the value delivered rather than replicating an existing design, you open up new approaches to addressing unintended consequences without compromising on delivery. In this case, the result is you no longer need the straw at all.

> **D:** So, really coming back to a core feature of the circular economy by focusing on value rather than the individual product and combining it with partnership approach as dictated by SDG 17?

K: Yes. When major consumer brands invest in circular solutions together, they are each better positioned to achieve their own independent goals around capturing the value of their products after point of sale, and incorporating post-consumer feedstock into those products. Everyone wins. One example of this is the Center's partnership with Starbucks and McDonald's. With these founding partners we launched the NextGen Cup Consortium to reinvent the cup to be 100% recyclable and compostable. The vision for this effort is to have many brands on board to reach a critical mass of consistent materials being collected, sorted, recycled, composted, and reused. The more retailers who join the stronger the effort will be to make processing easier at the infrastructure level. 600 billion cups are produced each year, so scaling the solution is a critical challenge.

Another Center effort I'm excited about is our partnership on an initiative bringing together apparel brands in a pre-competitive effort to standardise the type of data collected through embedded digital identification. The vision for CONNECTFASHION is that at any stage of the life cycle, you can scan an article of clothing and identify the brand, material, source, etc. and determine the best next path for reuse. Brands are already working on the digital technology, and we want to make sure there's a consistent universal framework, so the data can be leveraged to support circularity in the future.

D: When thinking specifically of SDG 17 and partnerships – how can cities and governments play a part and incentivise the creation of these collaborations? You mentioned that the U.S. doesn't have regulation at a national level, but is there movement in that direction?

K: We're seeing remarkable efforts at the local level. Cities and states are showing leadership and a recognition that a take, make waste system costs them too much money. For example, New York City spends about $60 million each year disposing of discarded clothing and textiles, even with textile recycling programs in place at a neighbourhood level. Much of this material has value on the resale market, and should be yielding revenue rather than drawing down taxpayer dollars. Municipalities see the negative consequences and costs of treating resources as waste, and have enacted local ordinances to address these issues. Some states and cities are adopting progressive bans on organics in landfills. There are plastic bag bans in many cities, however these often face powerful opposition at the state level. Seattle recently joined other municipalities in banning plastic straws. Ideally, local legislation aligns with consumer preferences—so that people don't see it as a sacrifice to consume in a different way—and corporations and emerging companies foster the innovation that's needed to create a new technology or design or business model that replaces that costly linear approach and serves everyone's needs, profitably.

D: What are the other types of partnerships that can support the transition from linear to circular?

K: At the Center for the Circular Economy our innovation partners include leading universities and trade associations who share our sense of urgency and interest in collaborative problem-solving. We don't want to replicate the silos we see in the linear economy. We're also building an international network of affiliated accelerators and incubators who share our goal of helping circular start-ups scale and commercialise their innovations.

D: What are you not yet seeing in the U.S. that you would like to see?

K: That's a pretty long list right now! I would be happy to see a wider adoption of material passports, transitions to modularity that enable design for disassembly, and mastery of the reverse logistics necessary for take-back and refurbishment programs. Also, the transition to product as service that Philips has pioneered so successfully in their municipal lighting contracts is not yet widespread. In their innovative business model, cities lease energy efficient lighting systems through a multi-year contract with low upfront costs, and accrue savings over time through lower energy costs, while Philips retains ownership of the products. By maintaining, replacing, and recycling components within the larger system, Philips recaptures some product value, and also benefits from continued ownership of all the data about the performance of their product. With the rise of e-commerce, strong secondary markets for electronics, furniture, and clothing, and the potential to scale growth without increasing reliance on volatile commodities, there are additional business opportunities with untapped revenue and I think we're going to see wider adoption in the coming years. In some cases, the interest is there but the technological and logistical challenges remain a barrier.

KATE'S BEST ADVICE FOR
PRE-COMPETITIVE PARTNERSHIPS

1. Make it win-win for all by identifying where the global shared solution will achieve a competitive advantage for each partner.
2. Highlight the need and opportunity for scale and the financial benefits that result.
3. Bring together the internal company teams focusing on innovation and technology with the internal company teams focusing on sustainability and circularity. In many cases the technologies or new approaches that are being innovated to solve an efficiency or supply chain challenge can be leveraged to support a more circular model.
4. Always think through the entire life cycle of your solution and how the product will get through every stage of our current systems and infrastructure.
5. Throughout the process question whether you're tackling the systems-level problem, without replicating a linear approach. Go big!

THE CIRCULAR CONSTRUCTION CHALLENGE

As we're writing and launching this book, the Danish philanthropic foundation RealDania is launching its global Circular Construction Challenge with Lendager Group as knowledge partner. The Circular Construction Challenge is calling for all innovators that promote waste as a resource. Material pioneers that either reuse, recycle or upcycle waste as new solutions and products in the built environment. The challenge focuses on circular economy and how the construction sector can reduce waste through intelligent use of resources for new building solutions. The challenge is a one-year process of rethinking waste, and a perfect opportunity for you to join forces with a partner and get going. More information on the challenge is found here: *circularconstructionchallenge.org*

PLASTIC FANTASTIC
– CROSS SECTOR PARTNERSHIPS
FOR CHANGE

Plastic is a relatively new material. Though invented in 1907, its international breakthrough didn't occur until the 1950s. Yet, by 2015, 8.3 billion metric tons of plastic[4] had been produced. If that number in itself is not worrying, consider that 75 percent of this plastic – more than 6 billion ton – has already become waste, 12 percent of which has been incinerated[6], while only 9 percent is recycled[5]. That leaves us with nearly 5 billion tons of plastic waste either piled up on landfills or spread throughout nature, with most of it completely unaccounted for[7]. From a purely economic point of view, this means that the global economy is missing out on €480-720 billion worth of plastic.

According to estimates, our oceans now contain 51 trillion plastic particles – outnumbering the number of stars in our galaxy by 500 times[8]. And there's more on the way. Every year, around 8 million tons of plastic waste will find its way into our oceans. The Ellen MacArthur Foundation predicts that if the current trend continues, by the end of 2050 there will be more plastic in the oceans than fish.

Think about that for a second.

The consequence? Here's just one example that speaks for itself. In April 2018, a 10-meter-long whale washed ashore in southern Spain. Cause of death? Plastic. Doing what a whale does best – swimming in the ocean – it had swallowed so much plastic (29 kilos of mostly plastic and other waste materials including an entire gasoline container) that it could no longer digest and process its food[9].

Having a material with the qualities of plastics at such a low price point is a truly remarkable technological achievement, and it has given us the opportunity to produce tools, goods and structures, that have benefited society as a whole. Parachutes, computers, incubators, sports equipment, lightweight vehicles, just to mention a few

4. Knapton, S., 2017. Plastic weighing equivalent of one billion elephants has been made since 1950s and most is now landfill. The Telegraph

5. Parker, L., 2017. A Whopping 91% of Plastic Isn't Recycled. National Geography

6. Parker, L., 2018. We made plastic. We depend on it. Now we're drowning in it. National Geography

7. The Economist, 2018. Only 9% of the world's plastic is recycled

8. UN News, 2017. 'Turn the tide on plastic' urges UN, as microplastics in the seas now outnumber stars in our galaxy

9. Gabbatiss, J., 2018. Plastic pollution killed sperm whale found dead on Spanish beach. The Telegraph

examples. Indeed, one might conclude that plastic has almost been too successful and is now on a trajectory of over-doing itself. And that is a major problem. Because more than any other man-made material, plastic tells the story of how, in our traditional, linear mode of operation, even great innovations and improvements can become unsustainable and problematic. Just as phenomenal a material as plastic has been to humankind, it has been devastating to our surroundings.

The case is that with plastic, just as with other major innovations from our transition toward industrialisation, we did not fully understand how to use it without harming both ourselves and our environment. Or perhaps, before now, we did not really understand that we needed to be careful about how we used it.

With the alarming prospect of going ocean-fishing and having a greater chance of catching a plastic water bottle than a mackerel, it is hardly surprising that we have begun to focus on the negative effects of plastic rather than its taken-for-granted advantages. Thus, questions are arising: Is plastic really that helpful? Can we replace plastic with other materials? Should I use a bag made from paper or a fabric when carrying home my groceries? Why can't plastic be recycled? The many pros and cons of plastic – based on whole and half-truths – are the subject of endless public debate; and the end-result is often just more confusion.

So how do we tame this two-faced by-product of industrialisation? How do we regain control of an innovation that is on a course of self-destruction?

While no universal answer exists, it is clear that need and demand for circular plastic packaging solutions are on the rise - with 10% of the global market already committed demanding new solutions. This brings about great opportunity to cater to this increasing demand by creating sustainable plastic solutions through circular value innovation.

Looking at plastic in a greater context, we understand that many of today's global challenges have become deeply intertwined.

One example being how the growing global population causes an increased need for food. However, every year, one third of the food produced for human consumption does not get eaten – it ends up becoming waste instead[10]. Producing the food, transporting and handling the food causes enormous amount of CO2 to be sent into the atmosphere. But the right packaging can prolong the life of food and thereby help prevent food scarcity and lower the percentage that ends up being wasted.

But is preserving food and ensuring its longevity enough to justify the increasing amounts of CO2-emissions and pollution? Obviously not. Yet, it demonstrates how difficult it can be for consumers to understand the costs as well as the benefits of a material, and how Sustainable Development Goals (SDGs) and global agendas can sometimes conflict.

Luckily, there is a way to avoid clashes between these two seemingly-oppositional forces. The circular way. By decoupling the negative effects of plastic – we can unite the goals of eradicating hunger, reducing greenhouse gasses and ensuring life on land and under water.

10. This adds up to 1.3 billion tons of waste a year - equal to US$ 680 billion in industrialised countries and US$ 310 billion in developing countries.

Food and Agriculture organisation of the United Nations (FAO), 2018. SAVE FOOD: Global Initiative on Food Loss and Waste Reduction

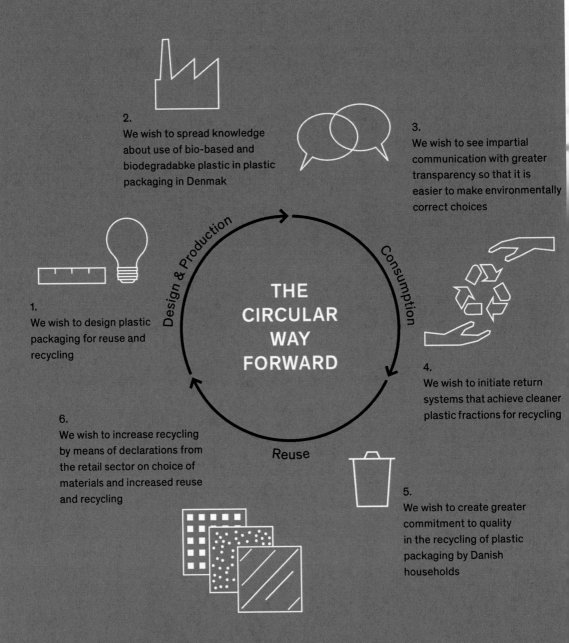

2.
We wish to spread knowledge about use of bio-based and biodegradabke plastic in plastic packaging in Denmak

3.
We wish to see impartial communication with greater transparency so that it is easier to make environmentally correct choices

1.
We wish to design plastic packaging for reuse and recycling

Design & Production

Consumption

THE CIRCULAR WAY FORWARD

4.
We wish to initiate return systems that achieve cleaner plastic fractions for recycling

6.
We wish to increase recycling by means of declarations from the retail sector on choice of materials and increased reuse and recycling

Reuse

5.
We wish to create greater commitment to quality in the recycling of plastic packaging by Danish households

In 2017, the government's Advisory Board for the Circular Economy issued a wide range of concrete recommendations for how Denmark can realise the potential of the circular economy. In this connection, the adcisory board describes the circular value chain as it is here. We have taken this illustration as our starting point and placed the recommendations of the forum for Circular Plastic Packaging in it.

THE VISION FOR CIRCULAR PLASTIC PACKAGING

From challenge to opportunity

Over the last half century, plastic production has risen by a staggering 2000 percent – from 15 million tons a year in 1964, to 311 million tons a year in 2014, and the demand is still increasing. In fact, the yearly amount of today is expected to double over the next 20 years – exceeding 600 million tons per year in 2038, if we do not change trajectory[11].

11. World Economic Forum, Ellen MacArthur Foundation and McKinsey & Company, 2016. The New Plastics Economy – Rethinking the future of plastics

The story of the dead whale is just one of many plastic horror stories the global population has been exposed to and, as we just explained, our awareness of the scope of the problem is rising. From an ecological perspective, global consumers are becoming increasingly concerned with the negative footprints their lifestyles leave behind.

Around the world, politicians and citizens are starting to take action to place more restrictions on plastics and packaging in particular. The corporate world is similarly moving ahead to respond to increased customer awareness and demands. At the World Economic Forum meeting in Davos in January 2018, eleven of the world's major Fast-Moving Consumer Goods companies, such as Evian, L'Oréal, Mars, M&S, PepsiCo, Coca-Cola Company, Unilever and Walmart, pledged to use only recycled, composted or reusable packaging by 2025.

On the political side, at the beginning of 2018, EU launched its program "European Strategy for Plastics in a Circular Economy," because, fortunately there *are* alternatives to the current damaging use of plastic.

First of all, we can start looking at what we use to produce plastic and start applying bio-based materials such as wood, algae, leather, corn starch, gut, cassava root and sugarcane instead of oil.

Second, we can use circularity as a tool to create materials, products and business models that make it economically attractive to collect and reuse plastic on a global scale. So here are the good news: 50% of the current plastic packaging can be recycled after making minor adjustment to the design and collection structures. Other types of plastics will take a little more effort as research shows that at least 30% of the current plastic packaging needs to be fundamentally redesigned in order to become recyclable (because of the difficulty of processing many different types of plastics when they are combined)[12].

12. newplasticseconomy.org

One of the biggest challenges to producing packaging that can be reused and recycled over and over again has been that no individual stakeholder can do the job alone. Only by coming together across the entire value chain can we create the road-map to future packaging.

CRITERIA / QUALITY	MAIN COMPONENT (container, bucket, tray, bottle, foil)	SUB-COMPONENT (closures, lid, inserts, seals)	DECORATION (cover, print, glue and labels)	EMPTYING (by consumer)	EXAMPLES
HIGH	Main component is in mono-material: PET, PE or PP. Shall tolerate washing to a suitable degree.	Sub-components are in the same material as the container or completely separated from the container in use.	Cover and labels are entirely removed in use or simple dismantling. There is no coloured print on the container, only on the cover or labels.	The packaging can easily be entirely emptied of residues after normal use. Only needs a light rinse with water (e.g. meat tray).	rPET can for example be used for new bottles, food trays and food tubs. rPE and rPP can for example become pipes, buckets or containers for non-food products.
MODERATE	Main component is of mono-material: PET, PE or PP. Or a minimum content of compatible material (cf. Appendix A). Main component is coloured.	Sub-components are not separated in use but are of materials that are compatible with the main component (cf. Appendix A). Sub-components are coloured.	Cover and labels are not separated from the container but are of the same material as the container or compatible materials (cf.Appendix A). There may be printing on the cover, labels or container.	The packaging is only partly emptied of residues after normal use. However sub-components are easily separated so that the consumer can rinse the packaging. (e.g. ketchup bottle)	rPET can for example be used for fibres for textiles. Can also be used for fleece sweaters blankets etc. rPE and rPP can for example become pipes, buckets or containers for nonfood products.
LOW	Main component consists of laminated materials that are not compatible (cf. Appendix A)	Sub-components contain incompatible plastic types, metal, paper etc. Sub-components are not separated in use.	Cover and labels are incompatible with the main components and cannot be removed. There is a great deal of ink printing on the packaging.	The packaging cannot be emptied of residues after normal use. (e.g. toothpaste tube).	Mixed plastic can for example be used for concrete filling, RDF and plastic to diesel.

That is exactly why we joined forces with the Danish Plastics Industry helping them form and drive the cross-value-chain initiative, the "Danish Forum for Circular Plastic Packaging." The Forum counts industry players, NGOs, political actors and others with a profound interest in seizing the potential of the circular economy[13]. We have been working proactively to develop an effective format and take the necessary steps to ensure the transformation to circular plastic packaging. But we must progress as a united front both inside and outside the forum. Thus, we have created a road map, highlighting the way forward for the industry as well as encouraging the political system to take action.

13. Forum for Cirkulær Plastemballage, 2017. Anbefalinger og handlinger

The first order of business was to set a new vision for the industry, and the forum has collectively made a commitment to work to fulfil the following vision:

DENMARK SHOULD BE A ROLE MODEL FOR CIRCULAR PLASTIC PACKAGING

1. Where there is an incentive to use plastic again and again
2. Where we design plastic products that provide value for society, consumers and the environment
3. Where the global plastic packaging solutions of the future begin

The vision for circular plastic packaging in Denmark is set. But only as a result of close cooperation among the various shareholders and an unwavering focus on action can success be realised. Only then does the Forum have the potential to change the incentive structure of the plastic value chain. The road to circular plastic packaging begins in the design process, and thus the forum created a design guide to increase recycling and reusability of plastic packaging. The design manual addresses the critical points about the producers' responsibilities regarding packaging. It not only encourages retailers to comply with the design manual's recommendation so that plastic packaging can be reusable and recyclable, it also serves as a direct input for the development of future laws and as a guide for how to procure sustainable plastic packaging solutions.

The plan is to revise it annually to include the development of new sorting and treatment technologies as well as new material types, such as recycled plastic.

As demand for cleaner plastic packaging increases and plastic packaging is being designed for reuse and recycling, larger quantities of cleaner plastic will be sent for recycling. This provides economies of scale in the recycling process, thus improving its economy.

The partnership prepared a business case for the collection of flower trays, buckets and straps that shows a financial gain for the individual retail store. In the longer term, when collection is expanded to include more plastic materials, the financial gains will increase.

Small pieces of shredded plastic at the Danish plastic recycling company Aage Vestergaard Larsen A/S.

The cross-sector participants in the Danish Forum for Circular Plastic Packaging.

Flower buckets are almost always made of PP, which is suitable for recycling. This will be maintained!

Straps are made from various materials and often each strap contains several different materials. The strap itself may be PS, the hook metal and the clamps PVC. A small number of the straps are made of only one kind of plastic and are therefore suitable for recycling, but these are usually sent for incineration. If each retail store only used one type of plastic - PS - for its straps, recycling would become much easier and more financially cost effective.

BUSINESS CASE FOR STRAPS, FLOWER TRAYS, AND FLOWER BUCKETS

Potential:

1. About 2,200 tons of plastic straps are scrapped every year in Denmark.
2. About 7,500 tons of flower buckets and trays are scrapped every year in Denmark.
3. By far the greater part of this total of 9,700 tons of plastic is currently sent for incineration.

Flower trays are produced from 3 different types of plastic which cannot be mixed together in a recycling process. On the other hand, each of the three types is suitable for recycling individually. If each retail store only used one type of plastic - PS - for its flower trays, recycling would become much easier and more financially cost effective.

If the products were systematically collected for recycling:

1. Earnings for the retail sector from sorting rather than incineration: DKK 500 per ton.
2. 9,700 tons of plastic recycled instead of incinerated = min. 30 jobs and turnover of > DKK 50 million.
3. 9,700 tons of reused plastic of a quality that makes it an alternative to virgin raw materials = 23,280 tons of CO_2-emissions saved.

HOW TO FUTURE-PROOF
YOUR BUSINESS AND PLANET
– a step-by-step guide

We hope we have given you information (as well as inspiration) which proves that change for the better is possible. Now, we hope to guide you from visionary ideas to measurable outcome, using our complementary tools and step-by-step guide to future-proof both your business and our planet.

Please check our website: *achangemakersguidetothefuture.com* for the latest updates and ideas.

THE STEP-BY-STEP GUIDE

1. Start by asking yourself: Why?
   a. What do you want to achieve and why? What is your purpose?

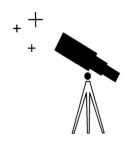

2. Spin the wheel of fortune! Use the *Circular Activity Wheel* to:
   a. Grasp the potentials of circular economy.
   b. Open both eyes and identify the blind spots in your company and industry.
   c. Look beyond your product: what is the real value you provide?
   d. Zoom in on your specific opportunities to change the game.

3. Reach for the stars but pick the low-hanging fruits first! Use the *Circular Opportunity Tool* to:
   a. Test your innovation and make sure that you start off on the right foot.
   b. Estimate your own business potential and how much is required to unlock it.
   c. Find your sweet spot! In most cases we recommend beginning with the assets that will give you a quick win and secure both internal and external engagement.

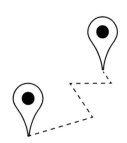

4. Check yourself before you wreck yourself! Use the *Business Model Canvas: The Circular Way* to:

   a. Start developing your activities (one BMC: TCW per activity – and one for an overview)

   b. Answer your WHY: what value do you create for your future users, the planet and the society at large?*

   c. Map your available resources – socially, culturally, financially, materially. Be aware of positive, unintended side-effects, turning challenges to opportunities.

   d. Map your value and supply-chain. What partners do you need? How do you involve and encourage them in your journey?

   e. Map your costs and revenue-streams and the connection between the two. From spending to earning: When will you start making a profit? Is there a delay? What can you endure given your current cash-flow?

   f. Map risks and barriers. What regulations are hindering your success? What habits do you need to break?

*Hint: you can get help for this part by looking back to step 1 and 2.

5. Is it worth it? Do the math: Is your innovation worth it:

   a. For people?

   b. For planet?

   c. For profit?

6. Have fun and get shit done!

   a. Decide how to tell your story

   b. Get started!

Step 1: Why?

Always start with the *why*. Why do you do what you do? What is your vision? Let's use Lendager TCW as an example. We set the vision, mission and purpose statement of the company back in early 2017. Our **vision** is to enable business and the environment to be each other's prerequisites. Our **mission** is to help our clients increase their value and competitive advantage, with the goal of accelerating the transition towards circular economy. This book is a clear example of the work we do.

It is important that you have a clear *why* and are aware of it to enable others to understand and relate to your vision. Because value innovation is not business as usual. Because being successful means being ready to change the rules of the game externally as well as internally. Because it means doing something new in your organisation.

Everyday businesses are successful at imitating current innovations and products or at optimising the existing ones, making them more efficient. But if you want to future-proof your business and leapfrog over your competitors by creating new markets and solving global problems, innovation is necessary. Imitation and optimisation is not enough. Making something new takes courage, willpower and leadership. It takes pioneers.

If you are not ready for value innovation, then don't attempt it. Just stick to optimising the solutions you already have. That way you'll at least do less bad. We don't say this to discourage you. We only want to make sure you are prepared in the best possible way. Plus, we want to do everything we can to make you succeed.

What do you want to achieve?
What is your dream with the innovation?

THE UNIQUE SELLING POINTS

These selling points are taken from a real resource-innovation done by Lendager TCW. The selling points represents your 'non-negotiables' – the factors you should always be able to deliver on.

GLOBAL SCALABILITY

The process for manufacturing the innovation is easy replicable, and the market for upcycled construction materials is growing worldwide.

AESTHETICS

The uniqueness of the input material and the production method gives the innovation a characteristic look not seen elsewhere, making it appealing on the market.

QUALITY

The product innovation is tested to have the strength and durability to function for at least 10 years.

ZERO WASTE TARIFFS

By upcycling a waste material the innovation will save up to 145.000 DKK in waste disposal tariffs.

BELOW BENCHMARK PRICE

With at sales price on 350 DKK per square meter, the innovation is just below the benchmarking price of similar products.

CO$_2$ SAVINGS

The project will save the environment more than 400 tons of CO$_2$ annually by taking on otherwise wasted resource and put it into new use.

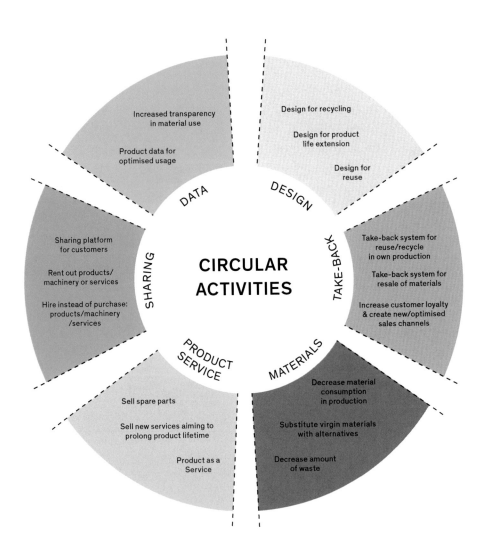

Step 2: Spin the wheel of fortune

Hopefully, you are itching to get started creating value innovation enabled by circular economy. So, here we share our strategies about how to take the next step in what we call the "ideation phase." Use our Circular Activity Wheel to get an overview of often-used circular economy activities. FYI: remember to keep an open mind. Use the tools for inspiration to get started; but don't let it limit you from thinking outside the box. Before prioritising the activities in our Circular Opportunity Tool, reflect on both your business potential as well as the resources you need in order make the right choices on your circular-economy journey.

2.1 QUESTION THE EXISTING!

What do you actually do? Start by looking at your value proposition: what are you providing? What is the real value you give our customers and how can you create a strategy to enhance that?

As we have already seen with Philips at Schiphol Airport: the company came up with a new non-product – *a service* – simply selling light to the airport via a subscription model, while keeping ownership of both lamps and light bulbs. Why does this matter? Because it created a new type of financial incentive structure, making it possible to increase value based on longevity and the quality of the innovative lamps. As we also saw, the Danish baby-clothing company VIGGA no longer sells clothes. Users subscribe to a service that regularly provides them with clothes for use during a specified time-frame, after which they are given back to VIGGA, to be checked, cleaned and recirculated. Here, the business model is the value innovation itself. As with Philips, VIGGA changed the rules by providing a product benefitting consumers and the planet while finding its own sweet spot between cost and value. Luckily, we see more and more of this kind of value innovation, but the innovation itself is nothing new. It was also what Phil Knight, founder of NIKE, successfully did back in the day when he introduced the company's future model. He is also doing it now, as when Nike started looking at modular shoe printing, and began using waste as a resource in their supply chain. In fact, 71% of all Nike's footwear today contain some sort of waste from their own production. Old Nike shoes, plastic bottles and manufacturing scrap have become a new material; Nike Grind - used to create new Nike products as well as sold to other partners who use it for playgrounds, gym floors and running tracks.

For a company to question what value it provides and then determine how to do it best is not new. What is new is that the circular economy has become the tool to create value innovation, benefitting not just people and increasing the profit, but also helping the planet.

Which brings us to our next point. Take the time to be inspired, to learn from others, not only within your own industry but also in alternative industries. What trends are happening and what innovations are being brought to market? Can you use some of these, from either a business-model or a technological perspective? Or in an entirely original way? You don't have to reinvent the wheel. Learn from others and build upon it to apply a new value within your area of expertise.

For that reason, it is always smart to use successful businesses as inspiration, so be on the lookout for interesting ideas, products, strategies happening elsewhere, to consider how (and whether) they might apply to you. By all means, prioritise an in-depth trend forecasting when setting on a new strategic journey.

Of course, we are well aware that there is *the perfect scenario* and then there is *the real world* with its daily struggles and resource constraints. This is especially true for small and medium-sized enterprises, where there is a huge potential for circular value innovation, but where resources, such as time, is a constraint. Doing R&D, while also working within an existing budget and trying to make ends meet, is not easy. Which is why we made time and resources key parts of The Circular Opportunity tool. For that reason, we have also kept this guide as brief as possible. In short, we want you to zoom in on:

What problem do you solve?
What value do you deliver?
What competitors do you outperform?
What do you benchmark with?

2.2 TESTING AND GROWING YOUR IDEA

Once you have identified your ideas and potential opportunities, the real challenge starts.

Before we get involved in the strategic-market exercises and business planning, we want you to start testing your idea. Create a 1:1 mock up. Make it tangible in whatever way you can and take it to a test market. Trust us: you won't regret this. In our experience, making your product development and thought-process tangible provides many strategic insights that benefit the entire business plan. We cannot recommend it highly enough.

What are you prioritising and how do you evaluate them? Start by getting an overview of the current business scene and know how your company and your products can or cannot be differentiated from your competitors and the rest of the industry. How would your idea benchmark? What are the measurable results?

Now, why did we just ask you to compare your company to the competition? Oddly enough, to make you shift focus from the status quo to alternatives! By looking at the normal way of doing business in your particular industry, you are seeing your blind spots. What value do you provide? How do you spend your resources? You need that information to break free and start focusing on the question: How can I do this better? Essentially, by evaluating yourself versus the competition you can redefine the problems. Much like Philips, when it realised that customers really wanted lighting rather than light bulbs and lamps, it changed to the circular product-as-a-service business model.

That is no easy task. You need to remember that – whether it is the product, the business model or the service – what you are proposing is different. If it was not, it wouldn't be a value innovation. The existing rules and structures were made for conventional thinking, and conventional thinkers. Being mindful of this alone can be a key element for your success.

Looking for inspiration?
Try: asknature.org

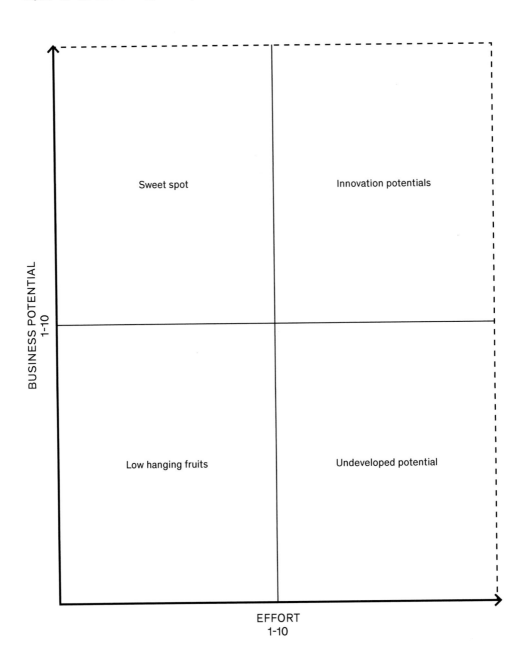

Y-AXIS BUSINESS POTENTIAL
How good is the business
potential concerning the specific
activity when it comes to brand
value, income, client relations,
cost savings etc.

X-AXIS EFFORT
How much effort must be put
into the activity before reaching
the goal: concerning investment,
work hours, skills, state of
market, new partnerships etc.

Step 3: Reach for the stars, but pick the low-hanging fruits first!

The Circular Opportunity Tool is a Matrix dividing the opportunities of the transition to circular economy into four categories: 1) Low hanging fruit 2) Sweet spot 3) Innovation potential 4) undeveloped market. These four areas are determined by two factors: 1) Business opportunity and 2) Resources needed .

The matrix allows you to easily test your innovation and assess if your expectation of potential and output matches the required effort to realise the idea. Making sure you start off on the right foot, and everyone onboard agrees to and are aware of the time it might take to achieve your first results - both financially and impact-wise.

Thus, a relatively low business opportunity combined with a low degree of effort enables you to pick the low-hanging fruits of the circular economy. If your idea, on the other hand, comes with a huge business opportunity with still just a little effort, you find yourself in the sweet spot. If your innovation poses a great market opportunity but first requires a lot of effort in terms investments, time, new competencies and market-readiness - it's placed in the area of innovation potential. A project that yet has little market opportunity but requires much effort should be considered in the area of an undeveloped market.

If you have more than one idea or innovation, the opportunity tool might help you prioritising which project to go along with first. In most cases we recommend beginning with the assets that will give you a quick win and secure both internal and external engagement. If you're still in doubt, we help you to find out if your idea "is worth it" in step 5.

But before going there, we ask you to "check yourself" and sum up your findings so far in step 4. For this task, we have redeveloped the traditional business-model canvas (invented by Alexander Osterwalder) changing it a bit and adding new elements such as answering why, mapping barriers and risks, and so on — all of which are even more relevant when you are doing something completely new. Finally, we ask you to finalise the business model canvas by prioritising the three most important actions you need to take.

We suggest testing and growing your idea by taking the next step, filling out the Business Model Canvas: The Circular Way. Make sure to stay focused on the value you deliver, what the customers appreciate you for the most. Challenge yourself constantly: Why am I choosing this and not that? Does this practice really create value, or am I choosing it by default because it is how things are normally done? Consider which activities or elements should be prioritised more, and which should be prioritised less. What should you stop doing all together? And what should you create? Always think across every aspect of your business and integrate the value innovation.

Step 4: Check yourself before you wreck yourself

When filling out the Business-Model Canvas – The Circular Way, there are a few things you should highlight and make sure you spend time on. These are:

4.1 KEY RESOURCES:

What do you have available internally and externally? In this section, we put particular emphasis on creating value by reactivating resources that are currently classified as waste. What we see – and what we have based the success of our production company Lendager Up on – is the huge potential in reactivating such resources as concrete, glass, bricks, wood, or plastic. Or as we do in Lendager TCW, where we help companies outside the built environment map their waste material, conceptualise potential new use, and create the innovation to bring the resource back to value.

Chances are that you, too, can recover resources from elsewhere and use them as your supply. Or perhaps you have dormant resources that you can reactivate in order to increase the value proposition of your innovation. In fact, we bet that this process of recovery and reuse does not only apply to new innovations. It is relevant all across your production line. In Apple's pilot test of its robot named Liam – whose task was to collect old phones – he managed to collect gold worth $40 million. If that amount of treasure was recovered in just a small pilot project, then imagine how many resources there must be out there waiting to be discovered?

One great example is SunPower, the American solar producer whom has transformed everything from their business models and factories to their disposal of waste, products and their employee job descriptions – all based on something they call CLEAN thinking. Even though you might imagine that the company's name suggests "clean" energy, it is actually about their philosophy of the future of business (it combines C for "circular finance," with LEAN – the business philosophy). The company's goal is to create the super-efficient factory where resource costs are significantly reduced. A key element of their strategy is reactivating un-utilised waste streams. This should ring a bell, as what they are doing is

Vision

The big why. What do you want to achieve?
What is your dream with the company/activity?

Value Creation

Look beyond your product: What value do you create for your future users,
the planet and the society at large? How can it be measured?
How will you create a compelling story about your value proposition?

Resources

Map your available resources - socially, culturally, financially, materially.
How might you build a multi-disciplinary team
within or across organisations to create value in
a circular economy?
What capabilities do you need to enable circular
flows and feedback mechanisms and run your organisation successfully in the short and long term?
Where will your resources come from (renewable or finite source) and what will happen to
them after use?

Activities

What activities might best help you achieve
your value proposition?
What might be the positive externalities
(i.e. the consequences of your actions on
others) of your activities?
And how might you monitor and design out
any negative externalities?

Get shit done

What's the first step you
should do tomorrow to get
going? In max 1-2 sentences,
explain why your value
innovation is needed and
what opportunities it brings.

Costs & Revenue

Map your costs and revenue-streams and the connection between the two. From spending to earning:
When will you start making a profit? Is there a delay?
What can you endure given your current cash-flow?
Could you shift from an ownership model of under-utilised assets to payment for access and usage?
How might you reduce cost volatility and dependence on the use of finite resources?
What can you do to mitigate risk?

Risks and Barriers

What barriers can potentially prevent a successful outcome of an activity (institutional, political, economic,
technical, etc.)? How can you overcome the barriers and what stakeholders or resources do you depend
on in order to succeed? When launching your initiatives what are the potential risks and how likely are they to occur?

Partners & Customer

What partners do you need?
How do you involve and encourage them in your journey? Who will be the main customers or users of your product/service? Who else might benefit from or will be affected by your materials/product/service?
Also consider beneficiaries beyond your immediate value chain and industry.
How might you connect customers with other parts of the journey of your product/service or materials?

Designing the Value Chain

How might you redesign your relationship with your supply chain?
How might you build feedback loops directly into your product/service that allow you to identify new opportunities?
What role could you play in the reverse logistics chain?

The Business Model Canvas tool was originally developed by Osterwalder & Pigneur. It is a widely used tool for developing commercial business models across industries. Business Model Canvas is particularly good at ensuring that all facets of a business model are considered in the development of a business. Lendager TCW modified the tool to adapt the model to the new conditions that the circular economy brings.

Is it worth it?

Do the math: Is your innovation worth it?
For people? For planet? For profit?
How might your business model help create other types of value? Human, social or natural capital?
How might new services increase revenue from existing products, assets or your delivery systems?

changing the rules of the game – now suddenly making buyers responsible for sales as well.

The CLEAN model demonstrates how circular economy is not just a tool to provide value innovation. It also helps to optimise conventional businesses and existing products, by reducing costs and freeing up revenue to finance value innovation.

But let's make one thing perfectly clear: It is not our intention to make you stop focusing on running your business as usual in the best possible tried-and-true way. Efficiency in the use of both materials and financial resources is still our core concern, and it is absolutely necessary. But if you want to survive and thrive as a business, future-proofing your business is not enough. You need to build value innovations on top of that, creating the solutions that bring us to the next level as a global society.

4.2 CUSTOMER RELATIONSHIPS (OR, AS WE LIKE TO CALL THEM, CUSTOMER PARTNERSHIPS).

Our experience is, that if managed correctly, circular economy is any marketing professional's biggest dream. This is particularly the case when circular economy is seen as a service and a resource recovery through take-back schemes, but it is also true in general. When you market a product as a service, you in fact integrate the user with your business – making it a continuous and valuable part of the customers' lives, increasing their engagement and giving them a sense of ownership. Why? Well, of course the subscription/service model does not create this sense of partnership completely by itself. We doubt there are many who have such a personal and positive feeling about, say, their phone company, even though they subscribe to one. Instead, telecommunications is market-driven by fierce competition. What changes the field is the value innovation, which includes not just the profit-margin and the benefit to individual user, but the advantage to the people and the planet as well.

Again, we can use VIGGA as an example, where data showed an extremely high engagement with current customers, making them extremely valuable in the business model as well as an important factor in attracting new customers. The key takeaway is ensuring

that the innovation not only creates value for the individual customer but for society in general.

4.3 RISK AND BARRIERS

Wouldn't it be lovely if information alone could achieve positive
goals and provide assurance to those who fear the new? No doubt
– to some degree – this is true. But our experience tells us that
much more is involved. We are talking about a systemic shift – a
radically new way of doing things. Which means that to succeed
you must be able to change behaviour and create a mindset within
your potential market and stakeholder group. You see, it is not just
you who is lowering the barriers and stepping onto new territory.
Your stakeholders and customers are too. And for them to do so
willingly, they must feel encouragement for and genuine interest
in your innovation and see the right balance between urgency and
opportunity. Strategic storytelling is a good way of highlighting
these goals.

Make sure you can prioritise your stakeholders in terms of who
is most likely to be moved? If they are your biggest adversaries,
don't waste your time there. Go for the folks with whom you have
positive and strong relationships. It takes courage and leadership
from you, but keep going, again and again. Every time you hit a
wall, find ways to turn it into an opportunity. Persistence will help
you overcome obstacles. Also, communications and stakeholder
management must be an integrated part of your strategy from the
beginning.

Always be able to explain why your
value innovation is needed and what
opportunities it brings – in max one
or two sentences.

4.4 FINDING YOUR GROUND AND PARTNERS

Normally, people are used to having rather static roles in their industry's value chain. It rarely changes more than a little over a long time. Yet, this doesn't have to be the case. Professionals who used to be involved in purchasing – and only responsible for that specific element in the value chain – are now taking on new roles as salesmen or entrepreneurs.

Another example from our daily life is demolition workers. As we explained in a previous chapter, many of them are now becoming important suppliers.

In a world where the only constant is change, our roles are indeed also changing! Your suppliers, customers are not as they used to be. In the case of Sunpower, the changed business model was an add-on, making the company more efficient. But it is possible that your role could change all together. That happened to a supermarket in Høruphav, Denmark, where – in collaboration with Danfoss, the world's leading green-tech company – the store was able to collect heat from its cooling system. Thus, instead of just floating up and into the air, the heat could be circulated to surrounding houses through the local heating system. In effect, this made the Høruphav retail store not just a supermarket but also a heat producer. Imagine if such system was implemented globally!

Anders went from being an architect to becoming the head of a group of businesses involved not only with architecture but also strategy and innovation consultancy whose goal is to produce recyclable materials for a regenerative world.

A last directive: Question those who make purchase decisions.

Who influences them?
What is the role of the end-user?
Who else adds value to the company?

Prioritise activating those individuals. If your solution helps to create local jobs by utilising local waste, talk to the local politicians. Make sure they are aware of your activity and the opportunities you can provide. Public servants may not be accustomed to the idea of circular economy and the change of roles in the supply chain. Which is why you need to let them know the upside, so they can set political targets in the procurement departments.

Opportunities for this type of added value in public procurement – where a purchase solves several issues without compromising on the initial delivery – exist throughout the value chain. For example, a Danish business Gamle Mursten ("old bricks" in Danish) collects, upcycles and resells discarded construction materials that can be reused individually, thus helping to reduce waste and CO_2-emissions. Moreover, it works with municipal governments to develop innovative public-private partnerships that provide jobs to citizens who have had a difficult time entering the workforce.

4.5 YOUR BLIND SPOTS:

Now we want to draw your attention back to the initial section of this book where we discuss Kant's notion of transcendental theory and the idea that we all have glasses through which we see the world. However much those glasses help us perceive reality, they are ineffective when it comes to envisioning the non-material universe. By this we mean the so-called blind-spots that all of us have. So, ask yourself, what are the things you cannot see and take for granted. Your answer will help you minimise the risk of being negatively surprised along the way to enlightenment and will maximise the possibility of your success in creating a value innovation.

Filling out the business-model canvas might take you back to the ideational state, and that's okay. It means your idea is improving.

Step 5: Final test: Is it worth it?

Now comes the time to check that you are, in fact, on the right track. To do this, you need to consider:

1. The costs of your R&D-processes required to make your innovation ready for the market.
2. How your production- and processing-costs per unit compare with benchmark prices per product or service.
3. Your innovation's value (environmental, social, economic) for society as a whole.
4. The potential scale of your innovation.

To quantify the above check-list, the following equation might help you assessing whether it is economically feasible to proceed with your innovation:

$$\frac{\text{Cost of R\&D (1)}}{\text{Potential scale (4)}} + \text{Cost per unit (2)} + \text{Required profit margin (3)} = \text{Benchmark price*}$$

*The numbers in brackets are references to the four points defined above.

If this figure is competitive with the price of existing solutions (or any potential solutions disclosed by your trend forecasting), you can proceed to the next equation.

$$\text{Potential scale} \times \text{Value of your innovation} = \text{Impact at scale}$$

See figure 17 for examples of how to calculate the different values created by your innovation. Remember to include the societal value of your innovation as well.

The potential innovation that passes the first test of being competitive with existing solutions and has the highest potential for societal value (the second equation) is the innovation to go with. That's because scale matters – in terms of both the total positive impact of your value innovation and your risk management. The bigger the demand, the easier it is to scale and achieve commercial viability. And, the bigger the business, the bigger the impact.

165
jobs created
per year

65.000
go to market cost
(USD)

7.800
tonnes CO2
reduced per year

83
revenue per item
(USD)

=

4.442
tonnes waste
reduced per year

329.000
units per year

27m
annual revenue
(USD)

Step 6: Have fun and get shit done!

Now it is time to make sure you keep reaping the benefits. As mentioned in the Klods-Hans section in *Part II*, a key element for success is being a great storyteller. The way we see it, it is of absolute importance that you are known as a change-agent working towards a regenerative future — benefitting people, profit and planet. So, continue to shout it from the roof, or whatever mode of communication you choose. People should always know your Why, and, if you need to tell them again, make sure you do it in a few short pithy sentences that your audience can relate to.

Understand the importance of building your brand as an entrepreneurial, pioneering effort that breaks down the traditional barriers of internal and external stakeholders. Moreover, clarify that your vision and determination to create a better world were inspired and enabled by your relationships with your customers , employees and strategic partners — and that you share this accomplishment with them.

Now, have fun and get shit done!

The choice is yours

"Remember to look up at the stars and not down on your feet. Try to make sense of what you see, and wonder about what makes the universe exist. Be curious. And however difficult life may seem, there is always something you can do, and succeed at. It matters that you don't just give up"

Professor Stephen Hawking

THE CHOICE IS YOURS

Thank you for choosing to read our book – it means more to us than you can imagine. It has been a great honour and a great pleasure to embark on this journey with you and to write this book. Completing the writing means opening a new chapter for us, and we hope the same goes for you. As with all journeys there are different roads to take and, thus, different choices to make.

So, we encourage you to be conscious of what you decide, as the results will guide your life and determine the kind of contribution you will make to your profession, to society and to your legacy. The good news is that you are already well on your way. Reflecting on the possibility of doing things differently – opening both your eyes, reading this book – are all are conscious choices. An indication of who you want to be, what you want your life to be like in the future and what you want your life to mean to the world around you

So, in this final chapter of this book, what we would like to talk about is, not surprisingly, *choices*.

A celebration of the ones you have already made as well as a celebration of the decisions and wonderful opportunities that await you. Opportunities that will enable you to make a positive difference in the world. You are lucky indeed – because, believe us – the world needs you! Because at the end of the day, while talk and books such as this can be valuable – what we need more than anything is action. Action from individual change agents who are questioning the current ways of doing things. We truly believe that, together, we can change things for the better. Create new ways of operating by challenging what we blindly considered the norm. And – can we let you in on a secret? – coming up with original way of doing things is good business and great fun!

What's more: Good business translates into jobs. So, if we had a crystal ball and could predict where the most jobs will be created in the not–so–distant future, we would answer that *regenerative business built on the principle is* a pretty safe bet.

But back to choices. Congratulations on choosing the path and doing the work to get you here. Because choices are not just about thinking and deciding; they are also about acting. Doing the work, standing up for what you believe in and getting this far, all suggest that you want to make a difference in the world. A difference in the environment, in the urban structures, for society in general and for people in particular.

HOW TO KEEP BOTH YOUR EYES OPEN
Our best advice to you is to make sure you have both eyes wide open. By being ready to learn and ready to question your previous beliefs – but also ready to see trends and opportunities in a new light. Combining skills, materials and schools of thought with an original point of view. Because life is about to change. Every day you will start realising that you are looking differently at the world and the objects, buildings and signs that surround you. This challenges not only you but the establishment around you as well. Which is good.

Be conscious about the choices you make. Don't decide anything just because it reflects the norm, or the traditional way. Don't accept that things have to be just the way they are and have always been. Realise that you have the ability and responsibility to design and create the future you want. It all comes down to the choices you make.

We imagine that making all these choices might sound daunting and scary. But it does not have to be. What it comes down to is your ability to listen to your gut feeling. Keep in mind that from time to time you will make the wrong choice. That is okay, because it is part of being human. What matters is how you handle your mistakes. That you learn from it, correct what you can, and get back to work.

And, sure, there will be lots of hard work and bumps on the road, but the feeling of having made the right choices is what will drive you on your journey, feeding you with passion, energy and love for the great opportunities in front of you.

We believe that the future of business will change the world for the better. We hope you will join us and the many other global citizens who are working around the clock to make positive change a reality. Open a newspaper any day of the week, and you will see the world needs us. The starting point is to see global challenges not only as difficulties to overcome but also as great opportunities. Believing that if we work relentlessly on finding solutions through innovation and cross-sector collaboration, we can transform problems into potentials. Potentials for society, for business and for each and every one of us.

So, we hope that every morning you will take on the responsibility of looking at yourself in the mirror and making the conscious decision to find solutions that can: regenerate nature, collect water, clean the oceans, clean the air, harvest clean energy, eliminate food waste, and convert waste to resources. Give people a roof over their head, access to energy and let them share and enjoy one another across generations, national borders, religion and colour.

By doing this, you can transform the global challenges of the past into beautiful, joyful, intelligent and healthy solutions for the future. Your future. The choice is yours!

On a final note, we want to leave you with this: Believe in yourself. Believe in your dream. But look for the nutrients that you need to grow. Just like a city, you are a metabolism yourself. So, believe in yourself but also have an open mind. Stand for the things you believe in, even when it is hard. Do the work, make the choices, and great things will follow.

We are all at the beginning of our journey. And we ask that you close your eyes and imagine:

A world with no resource scarcity
A world where waste does not exist
A world where our behaviour doesn't negatively impact our climate
A world where all people, regardless of where we were born,
are thriving

That world is real.
Let's join forces to make it happen together.

The choice is yours

Our guide to inspirational readings

1. Yvon Chouinard – Let My People Go Surfing
   – The Education of a Reluctant Businessman (2016).
   Penguin Publishing Group.
2. Alexander von Humboldt – Views of nature (1850).
   London, H. G. Bohn.
3. Andrea Wulf – The Invention of Nature: Alexander von
   Humboldt's New World (2015). Knopf.
4. Chris Zook and James Allen – Repeatability: Build
   Enduring Business for a World of Constant Change (2012).
   Harvard Business Review Press.
5. W. Chan Kim and Renée Mauborgne – Blue Ocean Strategy
   (2004). Harvard Business Review Press.
6. Phil Knight – Shoe Dog (2016). People's Press.
7. Thomas S. Kuhn – The structures of a Scientific Revolution (1962). University of Chicago Press.
8. F. Scott Fitzgerald – The Crack-Up (1945).
   New Directions.
9. Geoffrey West – Scale (2017). Penguin Press.
10. Julian M. Allwood, Jonathan M. Cullen – Sustainable
    Materials – With Both Eyes Open (2012).
    UIT Cambridge Ltd.
11. William McDonough, Michael Braungart – The Upcycle:
    Beyond Sustainability - Designing for Abundance (2013).
    North Point Press.
12. Peter Lacy, Jakob Rutqvist – Waste to Wealth: The Cir-
    cular Economy Advantage (2015). Palgrave Macmillan.
13. Elizabeth Kolbert – The Sixth Extinction: An Unnatural
    History (2014). Henry Holt and Co.
14. Adam M. Grant – Originals: How Non-Conformists Move the
    World (2016). Viking.
15. Ed Catmull, Amy Wallace – Creativity, Inc.: Overcoming
    the Unseen Forces That Stand in the Way of True Inspi-
    ration (2014). Random House.
16. The Ellen MacArthur Foundation, for continuous publica-
    tions on circular economy see:
    www.ellenmacarthurfoundation.org

NOTES: